Building Powerful Numeracy Facilitator's Guide

Pamela Weber Harris

Pam Harris Consulting LLC

© 2012 by Pamela Weber Harris

ISBN-13: 978-0-9853626-0-7
ISBN-10: 098536260X

Editor: Kim Montague
Production Editor: David Weber

dedication

To my husband, Daniel, who has been
with me through it all

contents

acknowledgements

A huge thank you to:

The good Lord, by whose grace all of this was possible.

My son, Matthew, for all of his help with the illustrations, layout, and the cover. And hugs.

My son, Craig, and my daughter, Abby, for their help and hugs.

My son, Cameron, for not failing out of BYU during the writing and his cyber hugs.

My husband, Daniel, for his support and hugs.

My cousin, David Weber, for wonderful editing.

Kim Montague, for reading, listening, suggesting, helping, and laughing at all hours.

Tim Pope, colleague and friend, for presenting with me in the early days and helping me get this project off the ground.

My brother, Mike Weber, for his InDesign expertise.

My parents for teaching me that I can do anything.

introduction

This facilitator's guide is a companion to *Building Powerful Numeracy for Middle & High School Students*. The intended audience is workshop presenters, teacher leaders, coaches, pre-service instructors, and anyone else who delivers numeracy professional development. This guide represents a compilation of workshops I have given to hundreds of teachers for over 10 years on developing powerful numeracy in themselves and in their students.

I wrote *Building Powerful Numeracy for Middle & High School Students* to help middle school and high school teachers to work better with their students. *Building Powerful Numeracy for Middle & High School Students* bridges the gap between the solid research at the elementary level and the secondary world, bringing secondary teachers the concepts, models, and strategies of numeracy.

Every year, as a secondary mathematics teacher, I taught students whose sense of numbers, arithmetic, and mathematics were procedural and memorized. When students did not memorize well, they came to me frustrated and discouraged. When students did memorize well, it was often difficult to get them out of the memorizing mode. Teaching students to reason and to justify their thinking was difficult, but worthwhile. With all of my work with graphing calculators, I knew there was a better way to teach algebra using relationships and connecting representations. When my four children started school, I began to search for a better way to teach arithmetic.

Each chapter describes activities, problem strings, and assignments for teachers and participants. The detailed lesson plans include presenter helps, such as discussion questions, sample dialogs, and detailed models. The beginning of each chapter has a handy "at a glance" section that displays the major big ideas, models, strategies, materials needed, and preparation for presenters. I personally use the detailed plans to prepare for each workshop and then use the two-page overview at a glace as my crib notes while delivering the material.

The video clips referenced can be downloaded from www.pamelawharris.com

CHAPTER 1 *one* 1

Addition

Addition

At a Glance

Materials

Blank paper, several sheets per participant

Large chart paper

Chart markers

Document camera

Projector

Graphing calculators, digit cards, or some way to generate random digits for the Close to 100 game.

Close to 100 game sheet, 2 copies per participant plus 1 copy for display

Big Ideas

Numerical relationships - not rote memory
Friendly, landmark numbers
Associative property
Magnitude, not digit oriented
Models and strategies are not the same thing

Models

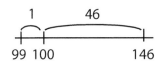

Strategies

Get to a friendly number
Partners of 10, 100
Give and take

Preparation

- Read Chapter 1.
- Read Chapter 2, p. 11-15.
- Read Chapter 3.
- Play Close to 100 so that you have your own understanding and experiences upon which to draw.
- Choose your random number generator for the game - calculators or cards.
- Ask several people you meet, "What is 99 plus anything?" and note their responses.
- Practice sketching models for each string.
- Work the Comparing Strategies problems on p. 37.
- Work the As Close As It Gets problems on p. 38.
- Work the Relational Thinking problems on p. 39.
- Read Appendix A: The Landscape of Learning.
- Read Appendix B: Algorithms.

Addition

At a Glance

Game: Close to 100

Model versus Strategies

$68 + 19$
$57 + 28$

An Over Strategy

$57 + 10$
$57 + 9$
$57 + 19$
$57 + 49$
$46 + 39$
$46 + 99$
$215 + 495$

p. 8

Give & Take

$99 + 47$
$99 + 29$
$1,997 + 2,989$
$7.98 + 2.19$
$5\frac{3}{4} + \frac{1}{2}$

p. 31

Give & Take

$48 + 26$
$139 + 52$
$2997 + 317$
$1.9 + 4.8$
$7.99 + 0.15$
$2.33 + 4.98$
$2\frac{3}{4} + \frac{1}{2}$

p. 32

Algebra Ending

Precalculus Ending

p.32

Doubles

$15 + 15$
$1.52 + 1.49$
$\frac{3}{2} + \frac{3}{2}$
$45 + 45$
$4.45 + 4.54$
$4511 + 4499$
$0.43 + 0.46$

p.36

Comparing Strategies
p. 37

As Close As It Gets
p. 38

Relational Thinking
p.39

Workouts

Addition
Detailed Plan

Close to 100

- Introduce the game
- Play a round with participants
- Participants play
- Discuss strategy
- Participants play
- Discuss game

1. **Introduce the game**
   Explain briefly that you will begin by playing a game so that you and the participants have a common experience from which to base the rest of the workshop. The game is called Close to 100.

2. **Play a sample round with participants** by randomly choosing 6 digits. Explain that their task is to use 4 of the digits to create two 2-digit numbers for which their sum is as close to 100 as possible. The score is the difference between the sum and 100.
   Demonstrate with a sample hand, such as: 5, 4, 1, 1, 6, 3.

			Sum	Score
54	+ 36	=	90	10
65	+ 34	=	99	1
61	+ 41	=	102	2

   Ask participants to find several possibilities and compare scores.

3. **Participants play**
   Have participants play several rounds. Circulate, and listen in. Look for participants who:

- seem to find the sums mentally
- are using the algorithm and writing each problem down.
- are jotting things down but not always the algorithm.

4. **Discuss strategy**

   Call participants back together and discuss strategy.

   How are you choosing from the 6 numbers?
   Are you focused on finding combinations of 10? 100?
   Are you looking to make 9's?
   Are you trying to make one really large number and one really small number?
   Are you finding 2 numbers close to 50?

5. **Participants play**

   Have participants play again considering other strategies that they just discussed. Circulate, and continue to look for different ways of thinking.

6. **Discuss the game**

   Call participants back together, and ask probing questions.

   <u>Place-value:</u>
   Can you use a 0 in the tens slot?
   Does that make it a 2-digit number?
   When does a 0 matter in a number?

   <u>Bringing out the difference meaning of subtraction:</u>
   Can the sum go over or should it be like we are playing "The Price is Right" where we can't go over?
   How would it affect the game if you used integers for the score?
   Would you have a score of -5 or +5 for a sum of 105?

   <u>Playing the game:</u>
   Why play this game?
   What age group could benefit from playing?
   Why?
   How?
   How does the game encourage reasonableness?

   <u>Differentiation:</u>
   How do wild cards add a level of abstraction to the game and allow students to generalize?
   How does the game let all students access the mathematics?

   A variation in the game is to find all of the permutations of a single set of 6 digits.

Models versus Strategies

- Model participant strategies for 68 + 19
- Discuss models versus strategies

1. **Model participant strategies for 68 + 19**

   Ask participants to find 68 + 19 and record their thinking.
   Circulate and find different strategies.
   Model several different strategies using an open number line, splitting, or equations. Restate participants' strategies as you sketch the models. Display the work, and keep it up to compare later. Bring out the following:
   - some strategies keep one addend whole while others split both numbers
   - the use of friendly (multiples of 10) or landmark numbers (25, 75, etc.)

   See the following examples:

If a participants says:	Model and restate:
I added 60 and 10 and that's 70. Then I added the 8 and 9, that's 17. So 70 and 17 is 87.	*You split up both numbers by place-value parts. Then you put the parts together.*
I added 2 to 68 to get 70, then I added the rest, 17, to get 87.	*So, you started with the 68, and kept it whole. Then you added 2 to get to a friendly number, 70. Then you added the rest, 17, to land on 87.*
I added 10 to 68, then 2 more to get 80, then 7 more to get 87.	*You also kept one addend whole, but you added a nice number, 10. Then you got to a friendly number, and then you adjusted at the end.*

If a participants says:	Model and restate:
I added 20 and then subtracted 1.	*You also kept one of the numbers whole, and you added a big friendly number, 20. But that was a bit too much, so you adjusted back by 1.*
I added 1 to 19 to get 20. Then I added the remaining 67.	*You also kept one of the numbers whole, but you kept the 19 whole! You got to a nice number.*
I added 70 to 19 to get 89. Then I subtracted 2.	*You also kept the 19 whole, but you went a bit over, adding too much. Since you added 2 too much, you adjusted back 2.*

2. **Discuss models and strategies**

- First, have participants look at the different "things" you've displayed to solve 68 + 19 and parse out the differences.

    What kinds of models do you see? [number lines and splitting models]

    What kinds of strategies do you see? [get to a friendly number; split both numbers into place-value parts, and put those parts together; add a friendly number]

    What is the difference between models and strategies?

- Discuss why the differentiation between models and strategies is important.

    How have we confused these terms and ideas in the past? [Many people treat the terms as if they are the same. It is more important for much of our conversation to know that you added a friendly number than it is that you used a number line. Once we know what the major strategies are, we can consider which work best for which numbers.]

- Discuss that representation is important in part because, now, many of your participants' cool mental strategies can be modeled, and thereby shared with their students more effectively.

Strategies: how you manipulate the numbers to solve a problem, ie. get to a friendly number, split both numbers by place-value parts, and put those parts together, give and take.

Models: how you display your strategy or the tools you use to solve a problem, ie. open number line, splitting.

Some teachers say, "Yes, let the students do their (inefficient) strategy because they finally get it!" They are so happy to have found success with the students, and they fear that forcing something else will ruin that. I'm not suggesting forcing something else or making the student abandon the meaning they have constructed. But I don't want to leave them in inefficiency either. Instead, I want to build on their understanding: always pushing for more efficiency and more sophistication.

Other teachers say, "No, absolutely don't leave them using inefficient strategies. Teach them the pinnacle of math—the algorithms—because that is the best way to do anything." But the algorithms are not the most efficient most of the time.

Ask both groups to keep an open mind as you work together.

- Discuss this sequence of modeling:
  - We start by modeling students' strategies so that they can see their thinking. This is a model of thinking.
  - As students get used to how their thinking looks on the model, they begin to transition to using the model as a tool to solve problems. This is a model for thinking.
- Discuss the idea of a hierarchy of strategies. Tell participants that, in this workshop, they will construct numerical relationships to develop a repertoire of efficient and sophisticated strategies.

  Which of these strategies do you think is the most efficient?
  Which of them is the most sophisticated?
  Is it ok to leave a student using a really unsophisticated strategy that the student really gets?

An Over Strategy

- **Deliver the Over Strategy string on p. 8**
- **Name the strategy, and post it**
- **Discuss "Problem Strings"**
- **Discuss the Landscape of Learning**

1. **Deliver the Over Strategy string on p. 8**
   Follow the example for delivering the string, p. 8-10.
   About halfway through the string, ask participants to draw number lines to model their thinking if they aren't already. As you circulate, remind participants to do the following:
   - to draw the line
   - to try to make jumps proportional
   - to try to record their own thinking not to just copy what you are doing
   Remember:
   - you honor participants' thinking by asking them to solve each problem however they want to
   - this is less about everyone sharing and more about you choosing which strategies to model
   - always include the over strategy

2. **Name the strategy and post it**
   Ask participants to describe the strategy that most of them were using by the end of the string.

   Turn to your partner, and describe what you were doing every time. Try to generalize the kinds of things you were doing.

Now, share with the group your generalization.
What could we call this strategy so that we can refer to this way of manipulating the numbers?
Post the name and an example problem on large chart paper.

Which problem in this string would you choose to represent this over strategy?

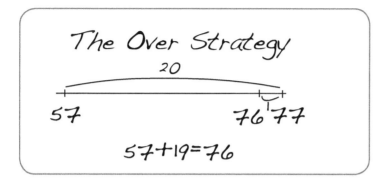

A problem string is a purposefully designed sequence of related problems that helps students mentally construct numerical relationships and nudges them toward a major, efficient strategy for computation. p. 7

Problem strings are not intended to be used all at once, handed out as worksheets, or used as independent work for students. p. 10

3. **Discuss "Problem Strings"**
   Have participants turn to p. 8 as you display the over string they just did. Point out the step-by-step help provided for delivering this string on p. 6-10.
   Discuss briefly the approach for delivering problem strings on p. 7. Reassure participants that they experience many more strings and that they will get the hang of what they are and how to deliver them to their students.

4. **Discuss the Landscape of Learning**
   Use the information in Appendix A: The Landscape of Learning to discuss the learning and teaching framework. In order to help students construct the big ideas, models, and strategies on the landscape, we need multiple entry/multiple exit lessons so that all students can access the math and all students gain. Since all students don't exit at the same level, we need to continue to offer such lessons.

Don't spend too much time here on talking about strings or the Landscape of Learning. Mention it here so that you can tag their experiences in the upcoming strings. Let your participants experience strings and the Landscape of Learning!

Single Entry	Single Exit	Multiple Entry	Multiple Exit

Notes:

Give and Take

- Ask, "What is 99 plus anything?"
- Deliver the string on p. 31
- Name the strategy and post it
- Do several problems from and then discuss the strings on p. 32
- Discuss the extensions for algebra, p. 33, and precalculus, p. 34
- Deliver the doubles strings on p. 36

1. **Ask, "What is 99 plus anything?"**
   Ask participants to discuss with a partner their ideas about adding 99 plus any 2-digit number.
   Ask for someone to volunteer their least favorite 2-digit number, like 47. (It seems that the least favorite numbers almost always have a 7!) Ask, "What is 99 plus 47?"
   Focus on the give-and-take strategy by modeling it as on p. 30.

2. **Deliver the string on p. 31**
   Use the classroom example on p. 30-31 to deliver the string.
   Model the last problem on an open number line:

   $5\frac{3}{4} + \frac{1}{2}$
   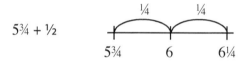

3. **Name the strategy, and post it.**
   Ask the participants to describe the strategy that most of them were using by the end of the string.

   > *Turn to your partner, and describe what you were doing every time. Try to generalize what kinds of things you were doing.*
   > *Now, share with the group your generalization.*
   > *What could we call this strategy so that we can refer to this way of manipulating the numbers?*

   Post the name, and an example problem on large chart paper.

   > *Which problem in this string would you choose to represent this give-and-take strategy?*

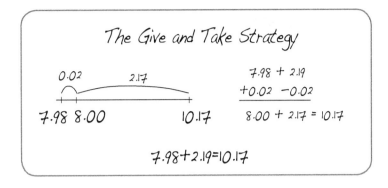

The Give and Take Strategy

0.02   2.17

7.98 8.00   10.17

7.98 + 2.19
+0.02 −0.02
8.00 + 2.17 = 10.17

7.98+2.19=10.17

4. **Do several problems from p. 32, and then discuss the strings on p. 32**

   Ask participants to solve a few more problems.
   Choose several problems from the strings on p. 32 based on your participants.
   Display the strings on p. 32.
   Ask participants to discuss in their groups the design of the strings.

   What kinds of numbers are in the strings?
   What kinds of problems?
   How do the strings progress?
   How are the strings different from each other?

5. **Discuss the extensions for algebra, p. 33, and precalculus, p. 34**

   Use the examples on p. 33 and 34 to work with participants through the algebra and precalculus endings.

   How would you generalize the give-and-take strategy using variables?
   What does the concept of friendly number have to do with radian measure of angles?
   How might the strings for the give-and take-strategy play out in real classes as teachers connect the numeracy work to current topics?

6. **Deliver the doubles strings on p. 36**

   Deliver both strings as per the example on p. 35-37.

Notes:

These problems are meant to inspire a conversation about the strategy to use based on the numbers in the problems. Encourage discussion.

So far, you have played a game, Close to 100, and done strings with participants. As Close As It Gets and Relational Thinking are 2 additional mini-lessons designed to help students to clarify their understanding. These lessons are meant to be short and can be used in those times that are too brief to do a string.

Relational Thinking problems are more and more important as participants and students learn more strategies. These problems help tease out the common attempt to surface memorize the strategies instead of constructing the understanding and relationships that allow the strategies to happen naturally.

Comparing Strategies

Give participants the 3 problems on p. 37 to work on.
Circulate, and observe.
Ask a couple of participants to display their strategy for each problem. Discuss. Focus the discussion on what it is about the numbers that influences their strategy choices.

As Close As It Gets

Introduce the activity using p. 38.
Display the questions on p. 38 one at a time.
Ask participants to quietly think about which answer choice is as close as they can get to the correct answer.
If time permits, ask partners to discuss their reasoning.
Ask a couple of participants to share their reasoning with the group.
Remember:
• Show each problem one at a time.
• Discuss each before moving to the next problem.
• Don't just round. That answer may not be the closest.

Relational thinking

Introduce the activity using p. 38-39.
Display the questions on p. 39 one at a time.
Ask participants to quietly think about the number that goes in the blank without computing. Instead, suggest that they use relational thinking.

Can you use relational thinking: how the numbers are related with that equal sign—to fill in the blanks? Don't compute! Don't "solve the equation", but, rather, use the relationships to find the missing number.

Have partners discuss their reasoning and then share with the whole group.
Discuss the true/false question.

Did you give and take the right amount?

Addition Participant Assignments

1. **Read Chapter 1.**
   Are you a "Kim" or a "Dana"? Describe your experience learning to compute. What parts of numeracy on p. 3 played a role in your experience? How do you think with numbers now?

2. **Read Chapter 2 p. 11-15.**
   Where do you see evidence of students' "digit approach" to addition in your classroom?

3. **Read Chapter 3.**
   Ask several people, including colleagues and students, "What is 99 plus anything?" Describe their responses.

4. **Play Close to 100 with your class.**
   How many of your students use the algorithm to add? How many use other strategies? What was the tone of your classroom as students played?

5. **Deliver the Over Strategy string on p. 8.**
   Be aware that you may encounter some resistance. Take note of those students who are wary—they may not trust that math can be anything but rote memorization. Some of these students may become your most ardent supporters when they realize that their way of thinking is actually encouraged. Take note of those students who are satisfied with doing everything the same way: with the algorithm. Push them to realize that they can be quicker, more efficient, and more flexible.

6. **Deliver several Give and Take strings, p. 31-32.**
   Do not expect that all students will start using the give-and-take strategy at first. Be patient. Allow students to solve the problems with their own strategies as you continue to model the give and take strategy. Comparing the strategies can cause disequilibrium, which gives students the opportunity to make shifts in their thinking.

7. **Intersperse the strings with As Close As It Gets and Relational Thinking problems.**

8. **Look for opportunities to give and take while doing the math at hand.**
   Force yourself to slow down and think about the numbers. Invite students to share moments of clarity when they apply numeracy and/or reasoning instead of rote memorization.

9. **Meet or beat the algorithm**
   Do you think you could always meet or beat the algorithm? If yes, invent addition problems for which you think you would meet the algorithm. If not, invent problems for which you think the algorithm is the most efficient strategy. Describe the numbers in the problems. Why do you think the algorithm works well for the problems? What kinds of addition problems do you think we could agree should be done with technology?

CHAPTER 2 two 2
Subtraction

Subtraction

At a Glance

Materials

Blank paper, several sheets per participant

Large chart paper

Chart markers

Document camera

Projector

Title a piece of large chart paper "Neither Problems" and hang in a place where participants can write on it.

Jordan 15 − 7 video

Speakers

Big Ideas

Two meanings for subtraction
Difference (distance) versus removal (take away, minus)
Constant difference
Implications for higher math

Models

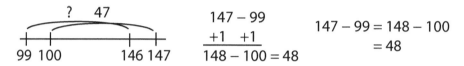

Strategies

Difference (distance)
Removal (take away, minus)
Constant difference

Preparation

- Read Chapter 1.
- Read Chapter 2, p. 15-28.
- Read Chapter 4.
- Practice sketching models for each of the strings.
- Ask several people how they would find 36 − 19 and note their responses.
- Look for real opportunities in your life to use the constant difference strategy. Be prepared to share your experiences.
- Work the Comparing Strategies problems on p. 49 on your own.
- Review the ideas from the "Implications for Higher Math" on p. 19-28. Be prepared to share them.

Subtraction

At a Glance

Difference vs Removal

$52 - 47$

$61 - 4$

$811 - 22$

$253 - 238$

$19.28 - 1.39$

$5.44 - 4.99$

$6\dfrac{1}{5} - \dfrac{3}{10}$

$8\dfrac{1}{3} - 7\dfrac{5}{6}$　　**p. 43**

Invent Problems

Ask participants to write a problem for which neither difference nor removal is necessarily more efficient.

Difference vs Removal

$m = \dfrac{y_2 - y_1}{x_2 - x_1}$

$\dfrac{3\pi}{2} - \dfrac{\pi}{4}$

$\pi - \dfrac{5\pi}{6}$

p. 44-45

Constant Difference

$65 - 29$

$62 - 26$

$71 - 35$

$63 - 27$

$66 - 30$

$70 - 34$

$76 - 40$

$132 - 96$

p. 46

Writing a Constant Difference String

$68 - 39$

$63 - 34$

$70 - 41$

$61 - 32$

$66 - 37$

$67 - 38$

$59 - 30$

p. 49

Constant Difference with Integers

$-7 - 13$

$-11 - 9$

$-4 - 16$

$20 - 0$

$-6 - 19$

$-12 - 15$

Implications for Higher Mathematics, p.19

p. 49

Comparing Strategies
p. 49

As Close As It Gets
p. 50

Relational Thinking
p. 50

Workouts

Subtraction

Detailed Plan

Difference—finding the distance between the numbers, counting up, adding up

Removal—removing one number from the other, subtract, minus, take away

Difference versus Removal

- **Deliver the Difference versus Removal string on p. 43**
- **Name the strategies and post them**

1. **Deliver the Algebra 1 Difference versus Removal string on p. 43**
Start the string with the context of sports scores for the first 2 problems.
As you relate the basketball scenario, write 52 − 47.

   It's basketball season, and the score at halftime is 52 to 47. We are losing. How much do we need to score to catch up?
   As participants answer, model the difference between 47 and 52.

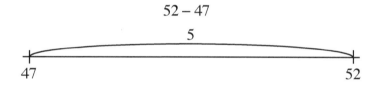

$$52 - 47$$

   As you relate the football scenario, write 61 − 4.

   It's football season, and the score at halftime is 61 to 4. We are losing. How much do we need to score to catch up?
   As participants answer, model the removal of 4 from 61.

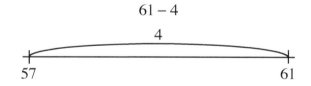

$$61 - 4$$

   Why didn't you use the same strategy for both problems?
   They are both asking the same thing; why not use the one and only "right" way: the algorithm?

Have participants turn to a partner and discuss the differences between the two problems. What about the numbers in the problems influenced them to do something different?

Ask participants to share. Generate the vocabulary as you discuss:

Difference: finding the distance between the numbers, counting up, adding up

Removal: removing one number from the other, subtract, minus, take away

Present the next two problems, $811 - 22$ and $253 - 238$ one at a time. After participants have worked the problems, model both strategies for each problem. Line up the models under each other for each strategy. If most participants use a difference strategy, model it first. Then ask everyone to try to use the other strategy. As you juxtapose the two strategies for the same problem, participants become more clear about why they want to use difference or removal depending on the numbers.

Difference—when the numbers are relatively close together, find the distance between them because the distance is small. Since they are close to each other, removing one would be like almost removing the whole number.

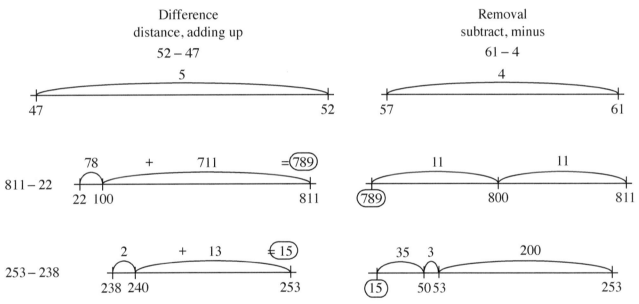

Ask participants to generalize when to use each strategy.

> *What about the numbers in a subtraction problem would nudge you to remove?*
> *What about the numbers in a subtraction problem would nudge you to find the difference between them?*

Continue with the last 4 problems in the string. Model only the strategy that makes the most sense.

Wait to have a conversation about the slope formula until the end of this section.

At the end of the string, focus participants' attention on the loca-

Removal—when the numbers are relatively far apart, remove the small one. Since the small one is relatively small, there is not much to take away. Since the numbers are far apart, it is cumbersome to find that much distance.

Chapter 2: Subtraction

21

Some participants may find the difference in a problem, such as 36 − 19 by going backwards from 36 to 19. Since they went backwards, they may mistakenly think they are removing instead of finding the difference. It is less important how they find the difference between 19 and 36, whether they count up or count back, and more important to acknowledge that the strategy was finding the difference.

If students start at 36, and remove 19, they are removing.

If students put 19 and 36 on the number line and find the difference between them, counting up or back, they are finding the difference.

tion of the answers. When removing, you start on the number line, remove the subtrahend, and end on the answer. When finding the difference, you start with both numbers on the number line, and the answer is on top of the number line (the distance between the numbers.)

2. **Name the strategies and post them.**
   Ask participants to describe the strategy that most of them were using by the end of the string.

   Turn to your partner, and describe what you were doing every time. Try to generalize the kinds of things you were doing.
   Now, share your generalization with the group.
   What could we call this strategy so we can refer to this way of manipulating the numbers?

   Post the name and an example problem on large chart paper.

   Which problems in this string would you choose to represent difference versus removal?

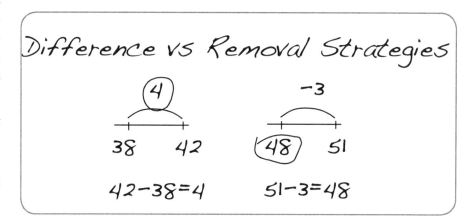

Notes:

Invent Problems

- Watch Jordan, 15 − 7
- Ask participants to invent a "neither" problem
- Have groups agree on a group problem and post
- After all groups have volunteered a problem, ask participants to look at all of the problems and find commonalities

FACILITATION TIP

It is important that participants can find the difference between the numbers in a subtraction problem because they will be finding the difference when they use the constant difference strategy.

1. **Watch Jordan, 15 − 7**

   Ask participants to watch a second-grade student, Jordan, who has been in a class where students have been using number lines to model addition and subtraction. The teacher was doing a research project, in lieu of being evaluated that year, and so the teacher was interviewing and filming the students. The students were given the problem live: no prompting or time to solve before being filmed.

   How would you describe Jordan's strategy?
   How would you model his strategy on a number line?
   Is he finding the difference or removing?

   Notice how Jordan moves his eyes as he 'sees' himself removing the 7 from the 15. Discuss that we can see how Jordan has developed a sense of space and of number relationships. He is also clear that his job is to figure out what 15 − 7 is, not to say "I don't know that one."

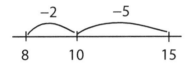

2. **Ask participants to invent a "neither" problem**

   Continue constructing the difference and removal strategies by asking participants to invent a problem for which neither strategy is particularly more efficient.

   So you are saying that you will find the difference when the numbers are relatively close together and remove when they are relatively far apart. To show me that you are really getting this, invent a problem for which neither strategy really wins. Find a problem where it wouldn't matter if you find the difference or remove because of the numbers in the problem.

3. **Have groups agree on a group problem, and post**

   After private think time, ask participants to agree on a problem as a group and then write it on a sheet of big chart paper that you have prepared.

I do not recommend spending time teaching "splitting" strategies for subtraction. Splitting by place-value is fine for smaller numbers for students who gravitate toward the strategy. However, if it doesn't come naturally for students, I have found that it is not worthwhile to force it.

The same is true for over strategies in subtraction. If students naturally subtract 39 by subtracting 40 and then adjusting, then continue to support them in this strategy. However, if it is confusing for students, I recommend bypassing this "over" subtracting strategy and going directly to the constant difference strategy.

The constant difference strategy is the goal.

4. **After all groups have volunteered a problem, ask participants to look at all the problems and find commonalities.**

Are all of these problems similar? How?
Are there any that don't fit? Why?

Neither Problems

64 − 29
101 − 57
752 − 368

Notes:

Difference versus Removal Extensions

- Do the extension problems for algebra, p. 44.
- Discuss the ramifications on the concept of slope
- Do the extension problems for precalculus, p. 45
- Discuss the strings on p. 43

1. **Do the extension problems for algebra, p. 44**

   Do the extension problems for algebra, p. 44.

   Ask participants to do the two fraction problems on p. 44.

   > *For which problem do you think in terms of removal? For which do you think in terms of difference?*
   > *How does this impact the way students work with mixed numbers? Do you have to "change to an improper fraction, subtract, then change back to a mixed number?" Or can you stay in mixed numbers when it makes sense? And change to improper fractions when it makes sense?*

2. **Discuss the ramifications on the concept of slope**

   Ask participants to discuss the impact of knowing only one meaning of subtraction (removal) on student understanding of the slope formula.

   > *Consider the slope formula. What do the subtraction signs mean? Minus and removal? Or find the difference, or distance, between coordinates?*
   > *What impact does it have on our algebra students when the only meaning they bring with them is the take-away meaning of subtraction?*
   > *How will students be able to understand better the rate of change as the ratio of differences if they understand the difference meaning of subtraction?*

3. **Do the extension problems for precalculus, p. 45**

   Ask participants to do the last two problems of the precalculus string on p. 43.

   > *For which problem do you think in terms of removal? For which do you think in terms of difference?*
   > *How does this impact trigonometry students when studying radian measure?*

4. **Discuss the strings on p. 43**

FACILITATION TIP

I am not suggesting that students never change mixed numbers to improper fractions. But it ought to be dictated by the numbers in the problems, not by some set procedure. We want students thinking, not only rote memorizing.

Display the strings on p. 43, and ask participants to discuss the strings and their impressions of subtraction so far.

Constant Difference

- Deliver the constant difference string, p. 46
- Name the strategy, and post it
- Represent constant difference with variable, p. 47
- Ask participants to do the Alaska problem, p. 19

FACILITATION TIP

If some participants see the pattern too soon, quietly suggest that they predict what some other problems in the string might be. Ask them to predict silently why you are asking problems that have the same difference. To what end is the string? Hopefully this keeps the few thinking while the rest are still engaged in solving.

1. **Deliver the constant difference string, p. 46**
   Tell participants that you are going to do another string in which they will have a chance to practice thinking about subtraction.
   As participants solve each problem, one by one, model a removal and a difference strategy. Line the removal strategies under each other and the difference strategies under each other. It is very important to line up the number lines for the difference strategies so that participants can see the differences shifting up and down the number lines.

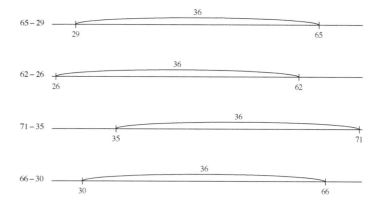

De-emphasize that the answers are all the same, 36. Try to keep people solving each problem as long as possible before they pick up on the pattern.

As soon as a critical number of participants begins to notice that each difference is 36, ask participants to look at the number lines representing the difference strategies.

> *Some of you are noticing that the answers to each of the problems is 36. What is going on?*
> *You might look at the number lines for the difference strategies. What do you see? Why?*

After you have discussed that the distance between the numbers has remained constant, if you have not already, give participants 66 − 30.

Of all of these problems, which would you rather solve?
How can you come up with another equivalent problem?
How can we use this idea to solve subtraction problems?

Give participants the next 2 problems in the string one at a time, 70 — 34 and 76 — 40. After participants have solved them, ask them to discuss which number they would rather make nice in a subtraction problem, the minuend or the subtrahend?

Finish with the string by giving the problem 132 — 96. Model on an open number line that 132 — 96 = 136 — 100.

Minuend—the starting amount

Subtrahend—the amount being subtracted

2. **Name the strategy, and post it**

Ask participants to describe the strategy that most of them were using by the end of the string.

Turn to your partner, and describe what you were doing every time.
Try to generalize what kinds of things you were doing.
Now, share your generalization with the group.
What could we call this strategy so that we can refer to this way of manipulating the numbers?

Post the name and an example problem on large chart paper.

Which problem in this string would you choose to represent this constant difference strategy?

The Constant Difference Strategy

3. **Represent constant difference with variables, p. 47**

Ask participants to use variables to represent the constant difference strategy. Use the example on p. 47.

How could you use variables to demonstrate the constant difference strategy?
In other words, if you start with a — b, how can you show the constant difference strategy? What are you doing to a and b?

4. **Ask participants to do the Alaska problem, p. 18-19**

Display the Alaska problem on p. 18-19.

Ask participants to find the difference and share their strategies with

FACILITATION TIP

Some participants may express that they are fine with removing or finding the difference, and they prefer to not use the constant-difference strategy. Encourage them to continue to work on the constant-difference strategy; they will need it when we get to some subtraction problems, especially within multiplication and division problems, and for decimal subtraction.

their groups.
Ask a participant to share the constant difference strategy. Discuss.

Writing a Constant Difference String

- Compare the strings on p. 18 and p. 46
- Discuss writing strings using p. 47-49

5. **Compare the strings on p. 18 and p. 46**
    Display the strings on p. 18 and p. 46.
    Ask participants to compare them and discuss in their groups.
    Have a short whole group conversation about the comparison.

6. **Discuss writing strings, using p. 47-49**
    Briefly discuss the string writing section.
    Emphasize that a good first step for teachers is to use pre-written strings, get used to those strings, and build teachers' own numeracy. Then, a good next step is writing strings. In other words, if a teacher wants to embark on writing their own strings, great! As a presenter, refrain from suggesting that teachers ought to be writing their own strings as a beginning step. Do not spend a lot of time on writing strings until teachers' numeracy and experience show they are ready.

Constant Difference with Integers

- Deliver the integer string, p. 49
- Discuss integer addition and subtraction

7. **Deliver the integer string, p. 49**
    Deliver the integer string making sure to line up the number lines so that participants can see the distances shifting.

8. **Discuss integer addition and subtraction**
    Use the information on p. 20-21 to discuss integer addition and subtraction.
    Have participants list the problem types for integer addition and subtraction. Show how students who have a good facilitation with the major addition and subtraction strategies and with modeling problems on a number line can do each of the problems just by doing them on a number line. When students have difference as one of the

meanings of subtraction, they can use that meaning as they approach integer subtraction.

Implications for Higher Math

Pam: "I didn't have to memorize all of that stuff—I could have understood it all!"

9. **Display and discuss the implications for higher math, p. 19–28**
   Discuss how many of the topics depend on the difference meaning of subtraction.

   How does facility with the difference meaning of subtraction influence the way that you look at each of these higher math topics?
   How might students see the distance formula and the slope formula as less procedural and more conceptual with an understanding of the difference meaning of subtraction?

Notes:

Comparing Strategies

Give participants the 3 problems on p. 49.

Circulate, and observe.

Ask a couple of participants to display their strategy for each problem. Discuss. Focus the discussion on what about the numbers influences their strategy choice.

As Close As It Gets

Introduce the activity using p. 50.

Display the questions on p. 50, one at a time.

Ask participants to quietly think about which answer choice is as close as they can get to the correct answer.

If time permits, ask partners to discuss their reasoning.

Ask a couple of participants to share their reasoning with the group.

Remember:

- Show each problem, one at a time.
- Discuss each before moving to the next problem.
- Don't just round. That answer may not be the closest.

Relational Thinking

Introduce the activity using p. 50-51.

Display the questions on p. 51, one at a time.

Ask participants to quietly think about the number that goes in the blank without computing. Instead suggest that they use relational thinking.

Can you use relational thinking—how the numbers are related with that equal sign—to fill in the blanks? Don't compute. Don't "solve the equation," but, rather, use the relationships to find the missing number.

Have partners discuss their reasoning and then share with the whole group.

Discuss the true/false questions.

Notes:

Subtraction Participant Assignments

1. **Read Chapter 1.**
    Are you a "Kim" or "Dana"? Describe your experience learning to compute. What parts of numeracy on p. 3 played a role in your experience? How do you think with numbers now? How do you do 36 − 19?

2. **Read Chapter 2 p. 15-28.**
    Where do you see evidence of students' "digit approach" to subtraction in your classroom? What is the most interesting application to higher math for you?

3. **Read Chapter 4.**
    Ask several people, including colleagues and students, "What is 36 − 19?" Describe their responses.

4. **Deliver the Difference versus Removal string on p. 43.**
    Be aware that you may encounter some resistance. Take note of those students who are wary. They may not trust that math can be anything but rote memorization. Some of these students may become your most ardent supporters when they realize that their way of thinking is actually encouraged. Take note of those students who are satisfied with doing everything the same way with the algorithm. Push them to realize that they can be quicker, more efficient, and more flexible.

5. **Deliver Constant Difference strings, p. 46, 49.**
    Do not expect that all students will start using the constant difference strategy at first. Be patient. Allow students to solve the problems with their own strategies as you continue to model the constant difference strategy. Comparing the strategies can cause disequilibrium, which gives students the opportunity to make shifts in their thinking.

6. **Intersperse the strings with As Close As It Gets and Relational Thinking problems.**

7. **Look for opportunities to use the constant difference strategy while doing the math at hand.**
    Force yourself to slow down and think about the numbers. Invite students to share moments of clarity when they apply numeracy and/or reasoning instead of rote memorization.

8. **Meet or beat the algorithm**
    Do you think you could always meet or beat the algorithm? If yes, invent subtraction problems for which you think you would meet the algorithm. If not, invent problems for which you think the algorithm is the most efficient strategy. Describe the numbers in the problems. Why do you think the algorithm works well for the problems? What kinds of subtraction problems do you think we could agree should be done with technology?

CHAPTER 3 three 3
Multiplication

Multiplication
At a Glance

Materials

Blank paper, several sheets per participant

Large chart paper

Chart markers

Document camera

Projector

Graphing calculators

Jordan 11 × 12 video

Angelica 11 × 17 video

Speakers

Big ideas

Single digit facts
Associative property
Distributive property
Counting strategies → additive thinking → multiplicative thinking and proportional reasoning

Models

1	100	50	51
68	6800	3400	3468

```
           16
       ┌─────────┐
   10  │   160   │
       ├─────────┤
    2  │   32    │
       └─────────┘
```

Strategies

Chunking
Larger, fewer chunks
Doubling/halving
5 is half of ten
Over and under
Using fractions and decimals

Preparation

- Read Chapter 1.
- Read Chapter 5, p. 52-62.
- Read Chapter 6.
- Practice sketching models for each of the strings.
- Ask several people how they would find 99 × anything, and note their responses.
- Look for real opportunities in your life to multiply in chunks using strategies that maintain magnitude. Be prepared to share your experiences.
- Work the Comparing Strategies problems on p. 84 on your own.
- Review the ideas from the "Implications for Higher Math" on p. 66-72. Be prepared to share them.

Multiplication

At a Glance

<table>
<tr>
<td>

99 times Anything

2 · 27

4 · 27

8 · 27

10 · 27

9 · 27

100 · 27

99 · 27

Proportional Relations

p. 74

</td>
<td>

Doubling/Halving

3 · 8

6 · 4

8 · 6

4 · 12

16 · 3

2 · 24

6 · 8

2 · 2 · 2 · 2 · 3

Find more equivalent problems

p. 77

</td>
<td>

Chunking

9 · 10

9 · 4

9 · 14

10 · 11

7 · 11

17 · 11

12 · 16

Distributive Property

p. 80

</td>
</tr>
<tr>
<td>

Over and Under

7 · 60

7 · 59

12 · 30

12 · 29

20 · 13

18 · 13

48 · 12

p. 81

</td>
<td>

Over and Under

499 · 1,000

499 · 999

60 · 40

61 · 39

p. 81

</td>
<td>

5 is Half of 10

28 · 10

28 · 5

15 · 28

42 · 15

42 · 16

150 · 52

145 · 52

81 · 149

p. 84

</td>
</tr>
</table>

| Comparing Strategies **p. 84** | As Close As It Gets **p. 87** | Relational Thinking **p. 88** |

Workouts

Multiplication

Detailed Plan

99 Times Anything

- **Deliver 99 times 27 string, p. 74**
- **Extend to proportional relations**
- **Single-digit facts**
- **Watch Jordan 11 × 12**
- **The importance of times 10**

FACILITATION TIP

Ratio tables are horizontal in the book solely for layout and printing. Alternate your use of horizontal and vertical ratio tables.

1. **Deliver the 99 times 27 string, p. 74**

   Deliver the string using the example on p. 74-75, modeling on a ratio table.

   As you go through the string, model the strategies on a ratio table as shown on p. 74-75. Keep the context in packs and sticks.

   End by eliciting from participants the generalization for 99 · *a* on the bottom of p. 75.

   > *Let's be general. What is 99 times anything? Think about it, and then share your thinking with your partner.*

FACILITATION TIP

The goal is to teach as much math as possible with as little rote memory as possible. This is a great example of how we can build from numeric work to algebra: multiplication in a ratio table to graphing direct variation.

2. **Extend to proportional relations**

   Use the example on p. 76 to discuss how the ratio table and modeling a proportional situation (27 sticks: 1 box) to work on multiplication also helps build toward proportional relations, their graphs, and their equations. When we teach direct variation, we can draw on this experience and build from it.

3. **Single-digit facts**

   Just as we want students to think through multi-digit multiplication, we can also have students reason about single-digit facts that they may not know automatically. We want the facts to be automatic at their finger tips, but, if they have to figure them, they should be trying to use multiplicative thinking instead of skip counting. We want to encourage multiplicative thinking over counting or skip counting (additive thinking.)

Talk through the following ways of reasoning about the single digit facts. Use the PowerPoint slide. These are my favorites, there are others. Note that these are transparent strategies, not tricks or gimmicks.

2 × anything: double
3 × anything: double + 1 group
4 × anything: double, double
5 × anything: half of × 10
6 × anything: double × 3; add 1 group to × 5
7 × anything: memorize 7 × 7, use other factor
8 × anything: double, double, double; or 2 groups from × 10
9 × anything: 1 group from × 10

Note that these transparent strategies work for these single digits times anything, not just another single digit.

> *So, these strategies work only for a single digit times a single digit, right? If not, give me an example of a multi-digit problem where we can use one of these strategies.*
>
> $8 \times 321 = 2 \times 2 \times 2 \times 321 = 2 \times 2 \times 642 = 2 \times 1{,}284 = 2{,}568$
>
> $9 \times 57 = 10 \times 57 - 1 \times 57 = 570 - 57 = 513$

4. **Watch Jordan 11 × 12**
    Have participants solve 11 × 12 using any strategy.
    Show Jordan, who is now in the middle of 4th grade, having answered 6 × 7 and finding 11 × 12. As you watch, ask participants to consider what he is thinking about. Note that he had just skip-counted to find 6 × 7, which is additive thinking, but we want kids using multiplicative thinking.

    > *How would you describe his strategy?*
    >
    > *What chunks did he use?*
    >
    > *Was he using a counting strategy, skip counting, or multiplicative thinking to chunk eleven 12's into ten 12's and 1 more 12?*

5. **The importance of times 10**
    Work with teachers to discuss the importance of times 10 as on p. 56. In order for Jordan to do that chunking strategy, he needed to know the strategy of times 10.

    > *What is 10 times anything?*
    > *If our students do not know what 10 times anything or 100 times*

FACILITATION TIP

When students answer, "I don't know," they think their job is to retrieve the fact from memory. Respond, "I didn't ask you if you know it. I asked you what it is. What do you know? And how can you figure it out from there?"

Counting strategies and additive thinking, p. 15

Making the shift to multiplicative thinking, p. 53

Using the ratio table to build proportional reasoning while building multiplicative thinking, p. 55.

A note on Jordan:
Jordan made a mistake when skip counting to find 6 × 7. This skip counting error shows all the more that we must encourage students to use multiplicative strategies and not additive strategies to find multiplication facts.

anything is, what can we do about it?

Ask participants to use an array to show why $23 \times 40 = 23 \times 4 \times 10$. Discuss with participants that students often think of 23×40 as 23×10 and then double to get 23×20 and double again to get 23×40. This is a fine beginning strategy, but we want to work with students so that they also think of 23×40 as $(23 \times 4) \times 10$. Students can then extend this reasoning to multiply by 400, 4,000, etc.

If your participants say, "You just add a 0 when you are multiplying by 10," help them to clarify their language by discussing that 23×10 is like 23 tens and you can write 23 in the tens slot, <u>23</u> __. That becomes <u>23</u> <u>0</u>, or 230. You are not adding a zero, you are writing 23 tens and no ones, 230.

Also, note that 10×23 can look and feel like a totally different problem. Use the commutative property and the array model to help students realize that $10 \times 23 = 23 \times 10$ and is therefore <u>23</u> <u>0</u>, or 230.

Notes:

Doubling and halving

- Deliver the 3×8 doubling/halving string, p. 77
- Do the extension for middle school: the Fundamental Theorem of Arithmetic, p. 78
- Do the extension for algebra: multiplicative identity and inverse, p. 79
- Display the geometry doubling/halving string
- Name the strategy, and post it

1. **Deliver the doubling/halving string, p. 77**

   Use the example in the book to deliver the string. Sketch all of the arrays in proportion, and emphasize the relationships of the changing dimension and area from one array to the next. Don't try to force the doubling and halving strategy. It will emerge by the end of this section. During this string, stress the relationships and the connections between factors, product, dimensions, and area.
   - As one dimension (factor) doubles, the area (product) doubles.
   - If both dimensions (factors) double, the area (product) quadruples.
   - If one dimension (factor) doubles, and the other one halves, the area (product) stays the same.

   An option is to hand out grid paper and have participants cut out arrays to demonstrate the relationships.

   Bring out the extension to scaling in geometry and measurement.

2. **Do the extension for middle school: the Fundamental Theorem of Arithmetic, p. 78**

   Use the example on p. 78 to explore the Fundamental Theorem of Arithmetic and prime factorization.

   Give participants the problems at the bottom of p. 78, and encourage them to use the strategy of rearranging the factors to see if they can find an easier problem: $6 \cdot 35$, $42 \cdot 35$.

   Emphasize again how a teacher can use numeracy to springboard into their secondary subject matter, building from numeric understanding and engagement.

3. **Do the extension for algebra: multiplicative identity and inverse, p. 79**

   Start the algebra doubling and halving string with problem $9 \cdot 5$ as shown on p. 79. Talk about tripling and "thirding" and quadrupling and "fourthing."

   Ask participants to explain generally how this works. Use the discussion on p. 79 to guide your work as you discuss multiplicative identities and inverses.

FACILITATION TIP

Arrays are always oriented as the number of rows by the number of columns, r x c, as in a 12 by 16 has 12 rows and 16 columns. This is consistent with matrices. The strings are purposely written for this orientation.

FACILITATION TIP

Closed arrays—

arrays with all of the grid lines drawn in; analogous to the closed number line.

open arrays—

arrays with only the outline drawn; analogous to the open number line

FACILITATION TIP

Try this one:

25×64

$= 50 \times 32$

$= 100 \times 16$

$= 200 \times 8$

$= 400 \times 4$

$= 800 \times 2$

$= 1{,}600 \times 1$

$= 1{,}600$

4. **Display the geometry doubling/halving string**

   Display the geometry on p. 77. If you have time, actually deliver the string. Discuss the relationships and how this string uses typical angle relationships (30, 45, 90, 135) as a way to springboard into geometry.

5. **Name the strategy, and post it**

   Ask participants to describe the strategy that most of them were using by the end of the string.

   > *Turn to your partner, and describe what you were doing every time. Try to generalize what kinds of things you were doing.*
   > *Now, share with the group your generalization.*
   > *What could we call this strategy so that we can refer to this way of manipulating the numbers?*

   Post the name and an example problem on large chart paper.

   > *Which problem in this string would you choose to represent this doubling and halving strategy?*

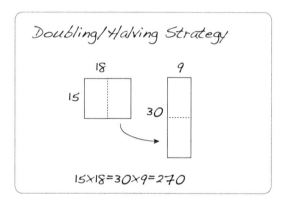

Notes:

Chunking:
The distributive property

- Deliver the chunking string, p. 80
- Show Angelica
- Solve 12 × 16 and post
- Discuss the traditional algorithm
- Display and discuss other chunking strings, p. 80
- Name the strategy, and post it

1. **Deliver the chunking string, p. 80**
   Use the example and arrays on p. 80-81 to deliver most of the chunking string for $9 \cdot 10$.

   After you demonstrate the problems $10 \cdot 11$, $7 \cdot 11$, $17 \cdot 11$, pause and reflect that participants just did a 2-digit by 2-digit multiplication problem in 2 chunks. This is a good moment to discuss how solving a problem, like $17 \cdot 11$, in manageable chunks promotes sense-making as students maintain the magnitudes in the problem. Surely, this is the best way to solve that problem, and this segues into watching Angelica.

2. **Show Angelica**
   Show the video of Angelica solving $11 \cdot 17$. This problem was given to 4th grader Angelica live with no preparation. She solves it in this way: $11 \cdot 17 = (11 \cdot 9) + (11 \cdot 8) = 99 + 88$. What is the significance of this? Angelica was new to the school. Her classmates had been working with numeracy for a few years. When she joined the class, she came with the algorithms for addition and subtraction, but she quickly recognized what was being celebrated in class: reasoning, justifying your choices, and searching for clever solutions. After the video stops, her teacher asks her how she would add 99 and 88. She lines up the numbers vertically and adds the 90 and 80 together, then the 9 and 8 together, and then added the 170 and 17. This shows that, even though she entered the class doing the algorithms well, within a couple of months, she was already trying other things to make sense of what is really going on: searching for more-efficient strategies.

FACILITATION TIP

What strategy could Angelica have used to find 99 + 88? How about give and take? 99 + 88 = 100 + 87 = 197.

3. **Solve $12 \cdot 16$, and post group solutions**
   Give the last problem of the string, $12 \cdot 16$. As participants solve the problem, circulate and find at least all of the strategies in Figure 6.10 on p. 81. Ask groups to post their strategies on chart paper and display. Ensure that at least 1 group shows the 4-chunk partial-product strategy. You might also encourage this strategy for those who know

12^2: $(12 \times 12) + (12 \times 4)$.

Have participants do a gallery walk.

Have each group explain their strategies.

If no one mentions it, bring up doubling/halving as a fine strategy.

If you have time, bring the associative and distributive properties at work as you generalize using variables, as on p. 81.

4. **Discuss the traditional algorithm**

   Ask participants to work together to use an array to find the algorithm, or, in other words, use an array to show the pieces or steps in the algorithm.

   As you circulate, if needed, help participants by suggesting that they do the algorithm in a modified way by writing all of the pieces down and maintaining place value.

   Discuss the connection between the partial product chunks and the non-transparent and compact algorithm.

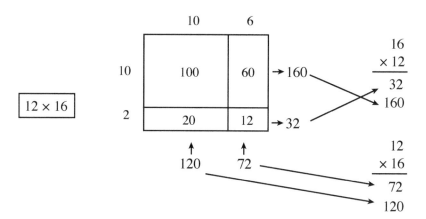

   Does this mean that our goal should be the 4-pane partial-product strategy because it is so transparent and it works all the time? [No, we can do 2-chunk solutions like Jordan did.]

5. **Display and discuss other chunking strings, p. 80**

   If you have time, deliver the other chunking strings on p. 80. If not, display the other strings, and discuss the pattern of the problems. Each string has sets of 3 problems; each has 2 helper problems to build the third problem. The strings end with a clunker problem; one where students have to create their own helper problems.

   Some participants may express the notion that solving the problems in the strings is not a real experience because, in the real world, students do not have the helper problems. Point out that the clunker problems are designed to help students find their own helper problems.

6. Name the strategy, and post it

Ask participants to describe the strategy that most of them were using by the end of the string.

> *Turn to your partner, and describe what you were doing every time.*
> *Try to generalize the kinds of things you were doing.*
> *Now, share with the group your generalization.*
> *What could we call this strategy so that we can refer to this way of manipulating the numbers?*

Post the name and an example problem on large chart paper.

> *Which problem in this string would you choose to represent this chunking strategy?*

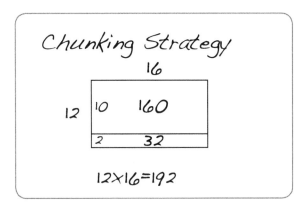

Notes:

Over and Under, Part I

- Deliver the 70 · 60 over and under string on p. 81
- Model the problems on a ratio table
- Name the strategy, and post it

1. **Deliver the 70 · 60 over and under string on p. 81**

   This string is written with pairs of partner problems where the first problem is easy but leads to the more difficult second problem. Participants have no need to draw the model of the first problem; but they can sketch it anyway so that you can use it to model removing the extra group or groups to find the second problem.

   Take note that, for the second set of partner problems, the array orientation is rotated. Maintaining the correct orientation allows you to see if participants arc just cutting off the same slice of the array each time or if they are reasoning correctly about wether they should remove rows or columns according to the numbers in the problems. After you finish with the string, point out the purposeful differing orientations of the arrays. Suggest that participants can use this to help them see how students are thinking.

   Note that, again, participants have solved 2-digit by 2-digit multiplication in 2 chunks.

   Discuss the implications for students as they apply this thinking with the distributive property in multiplying polynomials; see p. 81.

2. **Model the problems on a ratio table**

   Now, have participants work in their groups to model each of the problems in the string in a ratio table. Circulate, and ask scaffolding questions. Help, if necessary, to decide on which number the ratio table is based.

   What changes between the problems?
   What stays the same?
   Which group do you want to end up with?

   Bring the participants together, and discuss the ratio tables. Ask why they might want to use a ratio table instead of an array and visa versa.

1	70	69
9	630	621

1	4	40	39
13	52	520	507

1	60	58
12	720	696

3. **Name the strategy, and post it**
   Ask participants to describe the strategy that most of them were using by the end of the string.

   > *Turn to your partner, and describe what you were doing every time.*
   > *Try to generalize the kinds of things you were doing.*
   > *Now, share your generalization with the group.*
   > *What can we call this strategy so that we can refer to this way of manipulating the numbers?*

   Post the name and an example problem on large chart paper.

   > *Which problem in this string would you choose to represent this over-and-under strategy?*

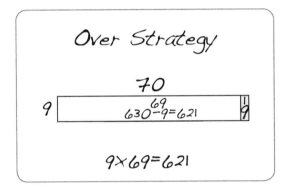

Over and Under, Part II

- **Deliver the 499 · 1,000 string**
- **Find the missing piece**

1. **Deliver the 499 · 1,000 string**
   This string is intended to push participants to clarify for themselves which group they are removing in the over and under strategy.
   Deliver the string by modeling on an open array.
   When you get to subtracting, remind participants that they can think through the subtraction. Help them model the subtraction on an open number line.

2. **Find the missing piece**
   Because the first partner problems begin with a 499 · 1,000, where one of the numbers is already friendly, this sets up the next problem as relatively easy to solve: just remove one group of 499 to get 499 · 999.
   However, the second set of partner problems starts with a problem where both numbers are friendly. This sets up the next problem

where both numbers change. Many participants will change both dimensions on the array without realizing they are missing a piece because they removed the same square unit twice. Have participants work together to figure out why some of their answers differ by just 1. If no one did the incorrect strategy as shown on p. 83, supply it yourself, and ask the participants to make sense of it.

5 is Half of 10

- Deliver the combined string in this guide, 28 · 10
- Play with the order by halving first
- Name the strategy, and post it

1. **Deliver the combined string in this guide, 28 · 10**
   Model these problems on a ratio table.

1	10	5	15
28	280	140	420

1	10	5	15	16
42	420	210	630	672

1	100	50	150	5	145
52	5,200	2,600	7,800	260	7,540

For the problem, 52 · 145, you could also solve it for fun:

1	100	50	2	52
145	14,500	7,250	290	7,540

Discuss that by these relationships allow you to work with numbers that are close to 5, 50, 500, etc. These relationships are very important in decimal multiplication.

2. **Play with the order by halving first**
   Challenge participants to generalize what they are doing when using the 5 is half of 10 strategy. Help them to see that they can change the order of the strategy: instead of multiplying by 10 and then halving, they can halve and then multiply by 10. Many times, it is easier to halve first and then multiply by 10 than it is to multiply by 10 and then halve the big number.

What are you doing every time?
If you are multiplying by 10 and then halving, can you reverse that order?
Why might you want to?
What property are you using?

$5 \cdot 420 = (10 \cdot 420) \cdot \frac{1}{2} = (\frac{1}{2} \cdot 420) \cdot 10$

3. **Name the strategy, and post it**

   Ask participants to describe the strategy that most of them used by the end of the string.

   Turn to your partner, and describe what you were doing every time.
   Try to generalize what kinds of things you were doing.
   Now, share your generalization with the group.
   What could we call this strategy so that we can refer to this way of manipulating the numbers?

   Post the name and an example problem on large chart paper.

   Which problem in this string would you choose to represent this 5 is half of 10 strategy?

5 is half of 10 Strategy

	18
10	180
5	90

15

15×18=270

Notes:

Comparing Strategies

Give participants the "times 68" problems on p. 85-86, the 4 problems on p. 86 to work on, and 999 · 887, 499 · 887 on p. 88, one set at a time.

Circulate and observe.

Ask a couple of participants to display their strategy for each problem. Discuss. Focus the discussion on what it is about the numbers that influences their strategy choice.

As Close As It Gets

Display the questions on p. 87, one at a time.

Ask participants to quietly think about which answer choice is as close as they can get to the correct answer.

If time permits, ask partners to discuss their reasoning.

Ask a couple of participants to share their reasoning with the group. Remember:

- Show each problem, one at a time.
- Discuss each before moving to the next problem.
- Don't just round. That answer may not be the closest.

Relational Thinking

Display the questions on p. 88, one at a time.

Ask participants to quietly think about the number that goes in the blank without computing. Instead suggest that they use relational thinking.

> *Can you use relational thinking—how the numbers are related with that equal sign—to fill in the blanks? Don't compute! Don't "solve the equation", but rather use the relationships to find the missing number.*

Have partners discuss their reasoning and then share with the whole group.

Discuss the true/false questions.

Notes:

Multiplication Participant Assignments

1. **Read Chapter 1.**
   Are you a "Kim" or "Dana"? Describe your experience learning to compute. What parts of numeracy on p. 3 played a role in your experience? How do you think with numbers now? How do you do 99 · 12?

2. **Read Chapter 5 p. 52-62, 66-72.**
   Did you think facts had to be rote memorized? What about your students? Which of the strategies is the easiest for you? Which is the most difficult?

3. **Read Chapter 6.**
   Ask several people, including colleagues and students, "What is 99 times anything?" Describe their responses.

4. **Take a few minutes to teach your students the single-digit fact strategies.**
   Ask your students how many facts there are that must be memorized. Have a few volunteer their least favorite fact. Discuss a couple of ways to figure that fact, quickly and correctly.

5. **Deliver the 99 times anything string on p. 74.**

6. **Deliver Doubling and Halving strings, p. 77.**

7. **Deliver Chunking strings, p. 80.**

8. **Deliver Over and Under strings, p. 81.**

9. **Deliver 5 is Half of 10 strings, p. 84.**

10. **Intersperse the strings with As Close As It Gets and Relational Thinking problems.**

11. **Look for opportunities to use each of the multiplication strategies while doing the math at hand.**
    Force yourself to slow down and think about the numbers. Invite students to share moments of clarity when they apply numeracy and/or reasoning instead of rote memorization.

12. **Meet or beat the algorithm**
    Do you think you could always meet or beat the algorithm? If yes, invent multiplication problems for which you think you would meet the algorithm. If not, invent problems for which you think the algorithm is the most efficient strategy. Describe the numbers in the problems. Why do you think the algorithm works well for the problems? What kinds of multiplication problems do you think we could agree should be done with technology?

CHAPTER 4 four 4

Division

Division

At a Glance

Materials

Blank paper, several sheets per participant

Large chart paper

Chart markers

Document camera

Projector

Jordan 1,188 ÷ 12 video

270 ÷ 18 videos (3)

Speakers

Big ideas

Divide by multiplying
The connection between division and fractions
Distributive property
Counting strategies → additive thinking → multiplicative thinking and proportional reasoning

Models

1		?
21		483

$$? \,\overline{)\,483\,}^{\,21} \qquad \frac{483}{21}$$

Strategies

Partial quotients (chunking)
Larger, fewer chunks
Over and under
5 is half of hen
Constant ratio

Preparation

- Read Chapter 1.
- Read Chapter 5, p. 63-66, 66-72.
- Read Chapter 7.
- Practice sketching models for each of the strings.
- Ask several people how they would find 270 ÷ 18, and note their responses.
- Look for real opportunities in your life to divide in chunks using strategies that maintain magnitude. Be prepared to share your experiences.
- Work the comparing strategies problems on p. 102 on your own.
- Review the ideas from the "Implications for Higher Math" on p. 66-72. Be prepared to share them.

Division

At a Glance

Multiply Then Divide

$21 \cdot 3$

$21 \cdot 20$

$21 \cdot 23$

$63 \div 21$

$420 \div 21$

$483 \div 21$

$308 \div 14$

Partial Quotients

p. 90

Partial Quotients

$18 \div 9$

$180 \div 9$

$198 \div 9$

$260 \div 13$

$39 \div 13$

$221 \div 13$

$299 \div 13$

$198 \div 6$

factor: $2x^2 - 5x - 3$

p. 95

Over and Under

$160 \div 8$

$168 \div 8$

$176 \div 8$

$152 \div 8$

$144 \div 8$

$240 \div 8$

$232 \div 8$

p. 97

Over and Under

$560 \div 56$

$504 \div 56$

$616 \div 56$

$1,120 \div 56$

$1,176 \div 56$

$1,064 \div 56$

$1,680 \div 56$

$2,418 \div 62$ **p. 97**

5 is Half of 10

$280 \div 28$

$140 \div 28$

$420 \div 28$

$360 \div 36$

$180 \div 36$

$540 \div 36$

$660 \div 44$

p. 99

Constant Ratio

$40 \div 2$

$80 \div 4$

$160 \div 8$

$320 \div 16$

$160 \div 16$

$320 \div 8$

$640 \div 32$

p. 100

Constant Ratio

$75 \div 3$

$150 \div 6$

$150 \div 3$

$300 \div 12$

$300 \div 6$

$600 \div 24$

$1,200 \div 24$

$600 \div 12$

p. 100

Constant Ratio

$60 \div 12$

$30 \div 6$

$15 \div 3$

$48 \div 8$

$24 \div 4$

$12 \div 2$

$504 \div 84$

$288 \div 36$

p. 100

Comparing Strategies
p. 102

As Close As It Gets
p. 102

Relational Thinking
p. 103

Workouts

Division

Detailed Plan

Multiply then Divide

- Ask participants to find 1,188 ÷ 12
- Show the Jordan 1,188 ÷ 12 video
- Deliver the Partial Products → Partial Quotients string, p. 90
- Discuss open and closed arrays
- Display the 5 is Half of 10 and Over and Under strings, p. 90
- Discuss "dividing by multiplying"

FACILITATION TIP

Don't give away that the division problems are the same as the preceding multiplication problems. Wait until most of the group notices. Then encourage participants to think about the division problems without looking at the counterpart multiplication problems

63 ÷ 21 = 3

dividend (area): 63

divisor (width): 21

quotient (length): 3

1. Ask participants to find 1,188 ÷ 12

Don't spend too much time here. Just ask participants to at least get a sense of the magnitude (size) of the answer.

To start off our division discussion, I'd like to ask you to do a quick problem. You can use whatever strategy you like. Don't stress. I just want you to have a sense of the size, the magnitude, of the answer.

2. Show the Jordan 1,188 ÷ 12 video

Introduce the video by explaining that this is the same Jordan they saw doing subtraction in second grade and multiplication in 4th grade. He had randomly been a part of bigger shoots. I purposely found him in 6th grade to shoot this video. As in the other clips, he had not heard this problem until you see him on the clip.

After you show the clip, acknowledge that the comma placement is problematic. Ask:

Why do you think he might have put the comma there? What might have influenced that? (He was thinking 12 hundred.)

We can deal with the comma problem because this kid is thinking.

What do you think about Jordan using multiplication to do this division problem?

How can we develop this kind of thinking and confidence? Hold on and take a deep breath because here we go.

3. Deliver the Partial Products → Partial Quotients string, p. 90

Deliver the string using open arrays as shown on p. 91. Remember to reiterate the location of each number in the first three problems:
- the factors are the dimensions
- the product is the area

As you finish the 21 · 23 problem, remind the participants that we can call this chunking of multiplication problems "partial products." Some may have heard the term "partial product" referring to the strategy of breaking the factors into their place-value parts, but "partial products" can refer to any chunking of the product.

When you get to 63 ÷ 21, ask the participants where these numbers go on an array.
- the dividend is the area
- the divisor is a dimension

Purposely place the **divisor on the top of the array** instead of the at left side. This helps participants continue to think about the problem instead of reverting to memorized procedures. Do not talk about this until you have finished with this string; just mention that, since you have to decide, you will choose to put it on top.

As participants solve the last problem, 308 ÷ 14, circulate and find participants who used a 3-chunk strategy (shown on the left of Figure 7.9, p. 93) and a participant who used a 2-chunk strategy (shown on the right of 7.9, p. 93). Have both participants display their work or explain their thinking as you model it.

FACILITATION TIP

In addition and subtraction, we seek for fewer longer jumps. In multiplication and division, we seek for fewer, larger chunks.

Remind participants that we want to know how they are really thinking about the problems and to encourage them to use fewer, bigger chunks. This is about building relationships among the numbers so that the strategies are natural extensions of thought; it is not about rote-memorizing each strategy.

Ask participants to look at the design of the string. Note that the string begins with partial products and ends with partial quotients. We can use strings like these to build the connections between multiplication and division.

4. **Discuss open and closed arrays**

   Briefly mention that you are using open arrays to model the multiplicative relationships. Students who have not yet worked with arrays, may need some experience with grid paper.

   Mention that you are placing the divisor on the top of the array on purpose. Explain that, by doing this, you are subtly encouraging them to think about the relationships among the numbers and not just performing memorized steps. See the discussion on p. 91-92 and Figure 7.6.

5. **Show the 5 is Half of 10 and Over and Under strings, p. 90**

Closed arrays—

arrays with all of the grid lines drawn in; analogous to the closed number line.

open arrays—

arrays with only the outline drawn; analogous to the open number line

FACILITATION TIP

You will be spending time on the 5 is half of 10 and over and under strings later so do not belabor them now.

If your participants have worked with you through the multiplication section of *Building Powerful Numeracy*, display these strings or work through them quickly.

If your participants have not done much work with multiplication numeracy, take some time to work through these strings to begin to build these multiplicative strategies. Focus on them as multiplication strategies rather than division strategies.

6. **Discuss "dividing by multiplying"**

   Ask participants to think metacognitively, to think about their thinking.

   I'd like you to think about what your brain was doing to solve these problems; be a bit metacognitive for a moment. Who would share how they were thinking about division perhaps differently than you have in the past?

   How do the chunks that we used in these problems compare with the chunks in the long division algorithm?

   Do not go into detail about the long division algorithm yet. Just raise the idea for now.

   Do not name any strategies yet. You will go into partial quotients more in the next string.

Notes:

Partial quotients

- **Deliver the 18 ÷ 9 string, p. 95**
- **Deliver the 400 ÷ 5 string, p. 95**
- **Display the 99 ÷ 9 string, p. 95**
- **Do the extension for algebra: Factoring Binomials, p. 95**
- **Do the extension for precalculus: Polynomial Long Division, p. 96**
- **Name the strategy and post it**

1. **Deliver the 18 ÷ 9 string, p. 95**

   Model these problems on an open array.

   On the clunker, 198 ÷ 6, circulate, and find 2 or 3 different partial quotients and model them side by side.

   Which of these chunks do you like the best for these numbers? Why? What do you like about them?

FACILITATION TIP

Remember to keep arrays proportional and encourage participants to do so.

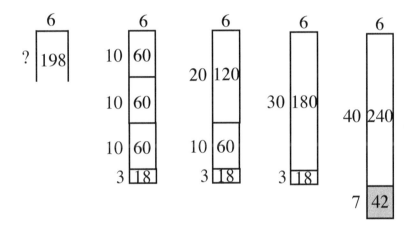

2. **Deliver the 400 ÷ 5 string, p. 95**

   Repeat the above with the 400 ÷ 5 string modeling on arrays and modeling several strategies for the clunker, 372 ÷ 31. At the end of the string, ask the participants a couple of questions:

   Does it free you up to be able to think in terms of chunks that make sense to you?

   The algorithm demands that you use the exact correct chunk every time, which results in students doing too many multiplication problems off to the side of their work. How is this method different?

   Some elementary programs advocate a similar method, where students can choose their chunks and feel okay to have a smaller chunk. We want to avoid leaving students choosing small chunks. Doing strings helps students develop numerical relationships so that they choose fewer, bigger chunks.

3. **Display the 99 ÷ 9 string, p. 95**

   Discuss the anatomy of all three strings in Figure 7.11, p. 95 using the paragraphs on p. 94. Suggest that participants consider delivering pre-written strings before they write their own.

4. **Do the extension for algebra: Factoring Binomials, p. 95**

   Remind participants that the array model, similar to algebra tiles, also works for polynomial multiplication. Depending on your participants' experience, you may want to review with them the "array-like" polynomial multiplication:

$$(x+1)(x-3) = x^2 + x - 3x - 3 = x^2 - 2x - 3$$

Have participants multiply a few polynomials using the "array-like" method.

- $(x-2)(x+7)$
- $(3x+5)(2x-4)$
- $(x-1)(x^2 + 2x + 2)$

Ask participants to look at their work and note where they combine like-terms as in this example:

$$(x^2 + 2x + 2)(x-1)$$

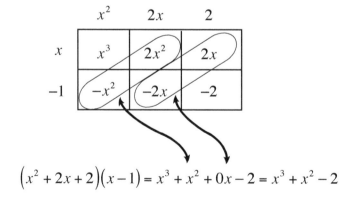

$$(x^2 + 2x + 2)(x-1) = x^3 + x^2 + 0x - 2 = x^3 + x^2 - 2$$

FACILITATION TIP

It's important for participants to note where they combine like terms because they need to recognize it when they factor or divide.

Suggest that they use the same strategy to factor polynomials as discussed on p. 67. Work through that example, factoring $x^2 - x - 6$, with the participants.

Have participants try another: factor $x^3 - x^2 + x + 3$

5. **Do the extension for precalculus: Polynomial Long Division, p. 96**
   Even better, polynomial long division can be done the same way. This is easier than factoring because you already have one of the factors. This is much easier than using the long division algorithm because you don't have to mess with subtracting polynomials and all of the accompanying sign confusion.
   Solve the example on p. 68 together: $(x^3 + 5x^2 - 4x - 20) \div (x - 2)$.
   If time permits, try these:
   - $(2x^3 - 5x^2 + 12x + 36) \div (2x + 3)$
   - $(3x^3 + 20x^2 - 22x + 5) \div (3x - 1)$
   What happens if there is a remainder? Try this:
   - $(3x^3 - x^2 + 7x - 5) \div (x - 1)$
   Why do we care about this? If you want to integrate that function, first you could do the division:

$$3x^2 + 2x + 9\ r4 \quad or \quad 3x^2 + 2x + 9 + \frac{4}{x-1}$$

   Then you can easily integrate each term.

$$\int \frac{3x^3 - x^2 + 7x - 5}{x - 1} dx = \int 3x^2 + 2x + 9 + \frac{4}{x-1} dx$$
$$= x^3 + x^2 + 9x + 4\log(1 - x) + c$$

6. **Name the strategy, and post it**
   Ask participants to look back over the strings you have done.
   Ask participants to describe the strategy that most of them were using by the end of the strings.

   Turn to your partner, and describe what you were doing every time.
   Try to generalize the kinds of things you were doing.
   Now, share your generalization with the group.
   What can we call this strategy to refer to this way of manipulating the numbers?

   Post the name and an example problem on large chart paper.

   Which problem in this string would you choose to represent this partial quotients, chunking strategy?

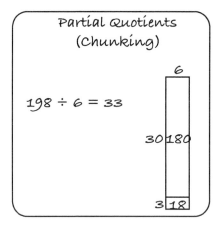

Partial Quotients
(Chunking)

$198 \div 6 = 33$

6

30 | 180

3 | 18

Notes:

Over & Under

- **If it helps, solve a multiplication string modeled on a ratio table.**
- **Deliver the 160 ÷ 8 string, p. 97**
- **Deliver the 560 ÷ 56 string, p. 97**
- **Discuss the traditional long-division algorithm**
- **Display the 120 ÷ 12 string, p. 97**
- **Name the strategy, and post it**

1. **If it helps, solve a multiplication string modeled on a ratio table.**
   If the participants have not done much work with multiplication in ratio tables, deliver a string that clarifies this concept. See the 99 · 47 string in the Multiplication chapter of this guide. Use a context, such as chewing gum sticks in a pack. Draw arrows on the ratio table, and write equations as participants describe their strategies.

   If a pack of gum has 19 sticks, how many sticks of gum are in 2 packs?

   $$2 \cdot 19$$
   $$4 \cdot 19$$
   $$8 \cdot 19$$
   $$10 \cdot 19$$
   $$9 \cdot 19$$
   $$5 \cdot 19$$
   $$15 \cdot 19$$
   $$100 \cdot 19$$
   $$99 \cdot 19$$
   $$50 \cdot 19$$
   $$49 \cdot 19$$

   Now ask some inverse questions without calling attention to the change. Just ask in context. Let the participants figure out what to do.

   If you have 228 sticks of gum, how many packs is that?
   If you have 969 sticks of gum, how many packs is that?

   As the participants use chunks from the ratio table you have been building, continue to model their strategies on that ratio table. See the following examples:

   What can you tell me about these last two questions?
   How are they similar to the previous problems? How are they different?
   The first few questions are represented by multiplication. How about these two? [19 · x = 228 or 228 ÷ 19) (19 · x = 969 or 969 ÷ 19]

As we solved these 2 division problems, staying in context and using a ratio table, did you feel a dramatic shift in the way you were thinking, or did it just follow like the previous problems did?
Acknowledge with participants that their use of very similar, if not the same, kinds of thought processes to solve the division problems that they used to solve the multiplication problems is noteworthy.

number of sticks of gum	19			228
number of packs of gum	1			?

number of sticks of gum	19	38	190	228
number of packs of gum	1	2	10	12

number of sticks of gum	19	76	152	228
number of packs of gum	1	4	8	12

2. **Deliver the 160 ÷ 8 string, p. 97**
   Begin this string by establishing the context of 8 yogurt cups in a box, and model using a ratio table. Use p. 97-98 as a guide.

   In our next string, let's change contexts. Let's say you're ordering yogurt for a class outing. You can get 8 yogurt cups in a box.
   Draw a ratio table, label it with (boxes, cups), and fill in (1, 8) as shown on p. 97.

   If I need 160 yogurt cups, how many boxes should I buy?
   Write 160 ÷ 8 to the left of the ratio table, and fill in the 160 in the ratio table as shown on the left of Figure 7.15.
   Continue the string in the same ratio table using arrows and braces to show the thinking of the participants.

3. **Deliver the 560 ÷ 56 string, p. 97**
   Model this string using arrays.

   Let's solve some more division problems, but, this time, I'll model them using arrays. So, if the first problem is 560 ÷ 56, where do these numbers fit on an array?

   Continue this string taking off a little or adding a little to the arrays. Limit the language in terms of dimensions and area.

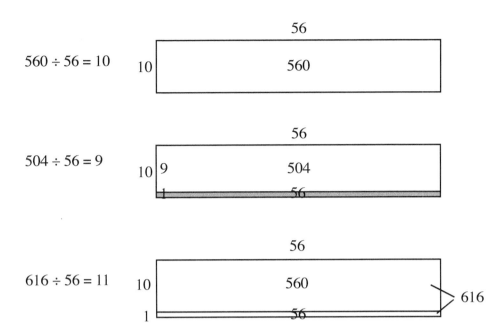

$560 \div 56 = 10$

$504 \div 56 = 9$

$616 \div 56 = 11$

For the last problem in this string, $1,680 \div 56$, the participants could use $1,120 \div 56 = 20$ and $560 \div 56 = 10$, but they could also use $1,518 \div 56 = 30$ and $162 \div 56 = 3$.

Add a clunker to the string: $2,418 \div 62$.

Ask the participants to look over the string and talk to a partner about the problems in this string and the strategies that you modeled.

What kinds of problems are in this string?

How would you describe the strategies we used to solve them?

How do these problems and strategies compare with the $160 \div 8$ yogurt cup ratio table problems?

Do not open this to the whole group yet. You will name the strategy soon, but this partner discussion will help the participants begin to think about it.

4. **Discuss the traditional long division algorithm**

Ask the participants to recall Jordan's $1,188 \div 12$ problem and to model Jordan's strategy on a ratio table and an array. Have them share with their table group.

Circulate, and find a couple of examples to display.

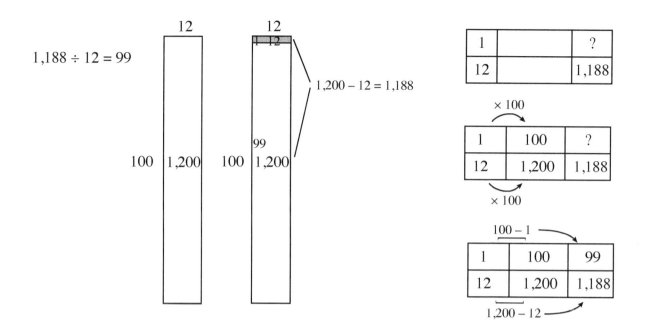

$1,188 \div 12 = 99$

$1,200 - 12 = 1,188$

Now, ask the participants to model the chunks in the traditional long division algorithm for $1,188 \div 12$ using arrays.

FACILITATION TIP

The "forgiving" adapted long division algorithm allows students to use smaller partial quotients than the exact partial quotients required by the traditional algorithm. It also keeps track of magnitude decently. However, it does not allow for the over strategy and it strongly suggests the subtraction algorithm. For these reasons, I do not advocate its use. A ratio table is much more flexible.

$1,188 \div 12 = 99$

$$\begin{array}{r} 99 \\ 12\overline{)\,1188} \\ -108 \\ \hline 108 \\ -108 \\ \hline 0 \end{array}$$

Does this mean that our goal should be to use the chunks of the algorithm? [No, we can do an "over" solutions like Jordan does.]

Can you do an "over" solution with the algorithm? [No]

Some suggest that we should do the "forgiving" adapted long-division algorithm. Should that be the goal? [But it does not allow for over strategies. All of the problems in the 160 ÷ 8 and 560 ÷ 56 strings would have had to be solved with more, smaller chunks.

Remember, our goal is fewer, larger chunks.]

5. **Display the 120 ÷ 12 string, p. 97**
   Ask participants to look at the 120 ÷ 12 string on p. 97 as you display it. Have each talk to a partner, comparing the three over and under strings.
   Discuss them briefly as a whole group. The purpose here is to guide the participants toward describing the strategy.

6. **Name the strategy, and post it**
   Ask participants to describe the strategy that most of them were using by the end of the strings.

   Turn to your partner, and describe what you were doing every time.
   Try to generalize the kinds of things you were doing.
   Now, share your generalization with the group.
   What can we call this strategy so that we can refer to this way of manipulating the numbers?
   Post the name and an example problem on large chart paper.

   Which problem in this string would you choose to represent this over and under strategy?

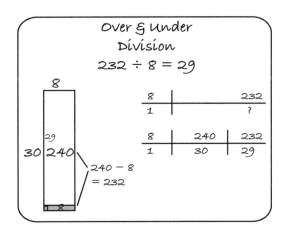

Notes:

FACILITATION TIP

The "forgiving" adapted long division algorithm, not preferred.

$$
\begin{array}{r}
9 \\
20 \\
40 \\
20 \\
10 \\
\hline
12\overline{)1{,}188} \\
-120 \\
\hline
1{,}068 \\
-240 \\
\hline
828 \\
-480 \\
\hline
348 \\
-240 \\
\hline
108 \\
-108 \\
\hline
0
\end{array}
$$

with brace: 99

another look:

$$
\begin{array}{r}
99 \\
12\overline{)1{,}188} \\
-120 \quad 10 \\
\hline
1{,}068 \\
-240 \quad 20 \\
\hline
828 \\
-480 \quad 40 \\
\hline
348 \\
-240 \quad 20 \\
\hline
108 \\
-108 \quad 9 \\
\hline
0
\end{array}
$$

Can't do the over strategy! Not preferred.

5 is Half of 10

- **Deliver the 280 ÷ 28 string on p. 99**
- **Show the 270 ÷ 18 videos**
- **Name the strategy and post it**

1. **Deliver the 280 ÷ 28 on p. 99**
   Model these problems in ratio tables and arrays as shown in Figure 7.20 on p. 99.

2. **Show the 270 ÷ 18 videos**
   These videos are of 6th grade students. I led a 5 is half of 10 string the day before, and I came back the next day to record video.

   Show each video one at a time. I asked the teacher to point out a range of students for the example. The first student, Haley, used a ratio table. The second student, another young lady, used equations. The third student, a young man, used a ratio table.

   > *What is Haley talking about with angles? [She used the relationship between straight angles, 180°, and right angles, 90°, to find half of 180.]*

   > *Why do we see the entries for 18 · 20 = 360 in the ratio table for the young man? [He tried doubling but found it was too big]*

   Give the participants a few problems from the other strings on p. 99.
   - 420 ÷ 28
   - 540 ÷ 36
   - 660 ÷ 44
   - 12,600 ÷ 84

3. **Name the strategy, and post it**
   Ask participants to describe the strategy that most of them were using by the end of the string.

   > *Turn to your partner, and describe what you were doing every time. Try to generalize the kinds of things you were doing.*
   > *Now, share your generalization with the group.*
   > *What can we call this strategy to refer to this way of manipulating the numbers?*

   Post the name and an example problem on large chart paper.

   > *Which problem in this string would you choose to represent this 5 is half of 10 strategy?*

VIDEO BACKGROUND

Just as I was about to video students, there was a bomb threat. So we all trekked out to the football field. Not to be dissuaded, after 30 minutes of waiting to go back to the classroom, I just decided to start the camera. I gave the students the problem, let them work it out, and then turned on the camera to get their explanations.

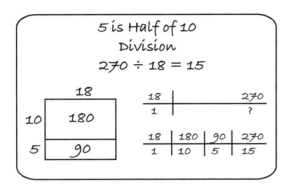

Constant Ratio

- Deliver the 40 ÷ 2 string, p. 100
- Deliver the 75 ÷ 3 string, p. 100
- Deliver the 60 ÷ 12 string, p. 100
- Give participants 1,188 ÷ 12 and 3,136 ÷ 64
- Name the strategy, and post it

1. **Deliver the 40 ÷ 2 string, p. 100**
   Model these problems on open arrays.
   Deliver the string based on the example on p. 100-101.
   Do not give away the constant ratio strategy in this string. Help the participants to develop the area and dimension relationships in these division problems and compare to the analogous relationships in multiplication.
   This string should go relatively quickly.

2. **Deliver the 75 ÷ 3 string, p. 100**
   Model these problems on open arrays.
   Deliver the string based on the example on p. 101.
   Encourage the use of money.
   At the end of the string, ask the following questions:

   Did these problems feel more partitive or quotative? Did you feel like chunking the dividend into 3 pieces, or did you feel like finding the number of 3s?
   What kind of thinking does the traditional algorithm always require? [How many divisor's gazinta (goes into) the dividend]
   What feels more efficient: to chunk 150 into 3 chunks or to find how many 3s go into 150?
   Does this mean that we always want to think partitively instead of quotatively? [No, we want the freedom to choose what works best.]

FACILITATION TIP

Partitive division: starting with the number of groups and being asked to find the size of each group (dealing out, sharing)

Quotative division: starting with the number in the group and being asked to find the number of groups (grouping)

See p. 63-64.

3. **Deliver the 60 ÷ 12 string, p. 100**
    Model these problems on open arrays.
    Deliver the string based on the example on p. 101.
    Build toward these generalizations:
    *   If you halve the area and one dimension, the other dimension stays the same.
    *   Likewise, if you halve the dividend and the divisor, the quotient stays the same.

    Using fraction notation, discuss the connection between division and equivalent ratios.

    > *What does the fraction bar mean when I write a fraction or a ratio? [It means division]*
    > *So, how might that influence your thinking if you write division problems in fraction notation?*
    > *Will that always help?*
    > *For what problems is this "finding equivalent ratios" strategy helpful? [When the dividend and divisor have easily seen common factors, it can be efficient to find equivalent ratios by dividing out the common factors.]*

4. **Give participants 1,188 ÷ 12 and 3,136 ÷ 64**
    Ask the participants to recall Jordan's solution to 1,188 ÷ 12.

    > *How did Jordan solve 1,188 ÷ 12? [Using an over strategy]*
    > *In light of your recent experience with these strings, how else might Jordan have approached 1,188 ÷ 12? [Using a constant ratio strategy]*
    > *Which strategy do you like the most for this problem?*

    Remember, this is less about which strategy is the best and more about having the freedom to choose between powerful, transparent strategies. This is also about having constructed the relationships that bring all of the connections on a problem to bear. This richness of thought, the breadth of connections, and the depth of understanding are the purpose for this exercise.
    Give participants 3,136 ÷ 64, and ask them to try several strategies.

    > *Discuss in your groups the strategies you like best.*
    > *Did you use a ratio table, an array, fraction notation, or some other model? Why?*
    > *What different ideas are embedded in the different strategies and different models?*

5. **Name the strategy, and post it**
    Ask participants to describe the strategy that most of them were using by the end of the string.

Turn to your partner, and describe what you were doing every time.

Try to generalize the kinds of things you were doing.

Now, share your generalization with the group.

What can we call this strategy to refer to this way of manipulating the numbers?

Post the name and an example problem on large chart paper.

Which problem in this string would you choose to represent this constant ratio strategy?

```
┌─────────────────────────────┐
│      Constant Ratio         │
│                             │
│    1,188 ÷ 12 = 99          │
│                             │
│   1,188 │ 594 │ 297 │ 99    │
│    12   │  6  │  3  │  1     │
└─────────────────────────────┘
```

Notes:

I call this strategy the constant ratio strategy because of it's parallels to the constant difference strategy for subtraction. In subtraction, if you keep the difference the same, you can use any subtraction problem to find the answer. In division, if you keep the ratio equivalent, you can use any equivalent ratio to find the answer.

Comparing Strategies

Give participants the problems on p. 102.

Circulate and observe.

Ask a couple of participants to display their strategy for each problem. Discuss. Focus the discussion on what it is about the numbers that influences their strategy choice.

As Close As It Gets

Display the questions on p. 103, one at a time.

Ask participants to quietly think about which answer choice is as close as they can get to the correct answer.

If time permits, ask partners to discuss their reasoning.

Ask a couple of participants to share their reasoning with the group.

Remember:

- Show each problem, one at a time.
- Discuss each before moving to the next problem.
- Don't just round. That answer may not be the closest.

Relational Thinking

Display the questions on p. 103, one at a time.

Ask participants to quietly think about the number that goes in the blank without computing. Instead suggest that they use relational thinking.

> *Can you use relational thinking—how the numbers are related with that equal sign—to fill in the blanks? Don't compute! Don't "solve the equation", but rather use the relationships to find the missing number.*

Have partners discuss their reasoning and then share with the whole group.

Discuss the true/false questions.

Notes:

Division Participant Assignments

1. **Read Chapter 1.**
   Are you a "Kim" or "Dana"? Describe your experience learning to compute. What parts of numeracy on p. 3 played a role in your experience? How do you think with numbers now? How do you do 2304 ÷ 48?

2. **Read Chapter 5 p. 62-72.**
   What is partitive division? What is quotative division? What are the implications that the traditional long division algorithm implies only quotative division? How might the constant ratio strategy impact the way you teach simplifying fractions?

3. **Read Chapter 7.**
   Ask several people, including colleagues and students, "What is 1,188 ÷ 12?" Describe their responses.
   Try the constant ratio strategy often. When is it most useful? When is it not so useful?

4. **Consider the division symbols.**

$$8\overline{)344}, \quad 344 \div 8, \quad \frac{344}{8}$$

   What ideas and models come to mind with the different notation? How might the notation influence the strategy you use? How can you build connections between the notations?

5. **Deliver the Connecting Multiplication to Division strings, p. 90.**

6. **Deliver the Partial Quotient strings, p. 95.**

7. **Deliver the Over and Under strings, p. 97.**

8. **Deliver 5 is Half of 10 strings, p. 99.**

9. **Deliver Constant Ratio strings, p. 100.**

10. **Intersperse the strings with As Close As It Gets and Relational Thinking problems.**

11. **Look for opportunities to use each of the division strategies while doing the math at hand.**
    Force yourself to slow down and think about the numbers. Invite students to share moments of clarity when they apply numeracy and/or reasoning instead of rote memorization.

12. **Meet or beat the algorithm**
    Do you think you could always meet or beat the algorithm? If yes, invent division problems for which you think you would meet the algorithm. If not, invent problems for which you think the algorithm is the most efficient strategy. Describe the numbers in the problems. Why do you think the algorithm works well for the problems? What kinds of multiplication problems do you think we could agree should be done with technology?

CHAPTER 5 *five* 5

Fractions: Addition & Subtraction

Fractions

At a Glance

Materials

Blank paper, several sheets per participant

Large chart paper

Chart markers

Document camera

Projector

Speakers

Jordan fraction addition video

Jordan fraction subtraction video

Big Ideas

It's all about equivalence.

Interpretations of rational numbers:

Part-whole comparison, measurement, operator, quotient, ratio

Models

$$\frac{1}{2}+\frac{1}{5}=\$0.50+\$0.20$$

Strategies

Fractions are quotients

Using money

Using a clock

Double number line equivalence

Equivalent ratios in ratio tables

Preparation

- Read Chapter 1.
- Read Chapter 8, p. 105-112, 121-24.
- Read Chapter 9.
- Practice sketching models for each of the strings.
- Ask several people how they would find ½ + ⅓ and ½ − ⅓, and note their responses.
- Look for real opportunities in your life to add and subtract fractions using strategies that find equivalent fractions. Be prepared to share your experiences.
- Work the Comparing Strategies problems on p. 142 on your own.

ddition & Subtraction

At a Glance

Fractions are Quotients

$3 \div 5$

$6 \div 5$

$6 \div 10$

$2 \div 3$

$2 \div 6$

$6 \div 9$

$3 \div 4$

Addition: Money

$$\frac{1}{2}+\frac{1}{4} \qquad \frac{1}{20}+\frac{1}{10}$$

$$\frac{3}{4}+\frac{1}{2} \qquad 2\frac{2}{5}+3\frac{1}{20}$$

$$1\frac{1}{4}+\frac{1}{10} \qquad \frac{1}{4}+\frac{5}{25}$$

$$\frac{1}{5}+\frac{1}{10} \qquad \frac{1}{100}+\frac{3}{25}$$

$$\frac{3}{10}+\frac{2}{5} \qquad \frac{3}{50}+\frac{3}{100}$$

$$1\frac{1}{4}+\frac{4}{5} \qquad \frac{1}{20}+\frac{1}{25}$$

p. 131

Subtraction: Money

$$\frac{3}{4}-\frac{1}{2} \qquad \frac{1}{2}-\frac{1}{25}$$

$$\frac{1}{2}-\frac{1}{10} \qquad \frac{3}{5}-\frac{2}{5}$$

$$\frac{3}{4}-\frac{1}{10} \qquad \frac{1}{5}-\frac{1}{100}$$

$$2\frac{1}{2}-1\frac{1}{10} \qquad \frac{1}{10}-\frac{19}{100}$$

$$5\frac{1}{2}-3\frac{3}{4} \qquad \frac{1}{50}-\frac{1}{100}$$

$$10\frac{1}{10}-9\frac{1}{5} \qquad \frac{3}{20}-\frac{3}{25}$$

p. 132

Addition: Clock

$$\frac{1}{2}+\frac{1}{3} \qquad \frac{1}{2}+\frac{1}{10}$$

$$\frac{1}{3}+\frac{1}{4} \qquad \frac{1}{15}+\frac{1}{4}$$

$$\frac{1}{3}+\frac{1}{6} \qquad \frac{5}{6}+\frac{1}{10}$$

$$\frac{1}{6}+\frac{1}{2} \qquad \frac{1}{20}+\frac{2}{3}$$

$$\frac{3}{4}+\frac{1}{6} \qquad \frac{1}{30}+\frac{1}{5}+\frac{1}{60}$$

$$\frac{1}{6}+\frac{7}{12} \qquad \frac{2}{15}+\frac{1}{30}$$

p. 134

Subtraction: Clock

$$\frac{1}{2}-\frac{1}{3} \qquad \frac{1}{2}-\frac{1}{10}$$

$$\frac{5}{6}-\frac{1}{2} \qquad \frac{1}{4}-\frac{1}{15}$$

$$\frac{11}{12}-\frac{5}{6} \qquad \frac{1}{6}-\frac{1}{10}$$

$$\frac{11}{12}-\frac{1}{6} \qquad \frac{1}{3}-\frac{1}{20}$$

$$\frac{5}{6}-\frac{1}{12} \qquad \frac{1}{5}-\frac{1}{12}$$

$$1\frac{1}{4}-\frac{1}{3} \qquad \frac{1}{2}-\frac{1}{30}$$

p. 135

Choose Your Model

$$\frac{1}{4}+\frac{2}{3}$$

$$\frac{5}{6}-\frac{1}{3}$$

$$\frac{2}{3}+\frac{1}{6}$$

$$\frac{1}{5}+\frac{3}{10}$$

$$\frac{3}{4}-\frac{1}{20}$$

$$\frac{1}{2}+\frac{31}{60}$$

$$\frac{51}{100}-\frac{1}{4}$$

p. 137

Choose Your Denominator

$$\frac{1}{5}+\frac{1}{7}$$

$$\frac{2}{7}+\frac{3}{5}$$

$$\frac{1}{3}-\frac{1}{8}$$

$$\frac{2}{3}-\frac{3}{8}$$

$$\frac{1}{4}+\frac{1}{9}$$

$$\frac{3}{4}+\frac{2}{9}$$

$$\frac{2}{5}-\frac{1}{15}$$

p. 137

Choose Your Denominator

$$\frac{1}{2}+\frac{1}{3}+\frac{1}{4}$$

$$\frac{1}{5}+\frac{1}{10}+\frac{1}{100}$$

$$\frac{1}{5}+\frac{1}{6}+\frac{1}{2}$$

$$\frac{1}{24}+\frac{1}{12}+\frac{1}{6}$$

p. 137

Comparing Strategies

p. 102

As Close As It Gets

p. 102

Relational Thinking

p. 103

Workouts

Fractions: Addition & Subtraction

FACILITATION TIP

Many participants may have only a part-whole understanding of fractions.

Some participants may have memorized that, to find a decimal equivalent of a fraction, they must divide the numerator by the denominator.

This is not sufficient.

Encourage the participants to develop the quotient meaning of fractions by staying in context with the money sharing problems and actually doing the division. When they share $4 among 10 people, they find that the share is really $0.40, which is 4 dimes out of 10 dimes or 4/10.

The quotient meaning is connected to the part-whole meaning, and both are important.

Detailed Plan

Fractions are Quotients

- Discuss the 5 interpretations of rational numbers, p. 106-107
- Display and discuss the $5 ÷ 10 string, p. 107
- Display and discuss the $10 ÷ 5 string, p. 107
- Deliver the $3 ÷ 5 string, p. 107

1. **Discuss the 5 interpretations of rational numbers, p. 106-107**
   Briefly point out the 5 interpretations of rational numbers. Explain that these meanings will come up and you will point them out as they do during the training. The first set of strings will work to develop the quotient meaning of fractions.

2. **Display and discuss the $5 ÷ 10 string, p. 107**
   Have the participants look at the string. Discuss that the string is designed to have students answer fair sharing questions in the context of people splitting money.
   The teacher asks each question in context, "How much money does each person pay if 10 people need to pay $5?
   The teacher would write, "$5 ÷ 10".
   After students give the answer, the teacher writes the following:
   $$\$5 \div 10 = \$0.50 = {}^5/_{10} = 0.5$$
   Have teachers discuss the possible conclusions on p. 108.

3. **Display and discuss the $10 ÷ 5 string, p. 107**
   Have the participants look at the string , have them quietly write out the answer to each problem, and discuss the generalizations that division of whole numbers can result in a whole number or a fraction between 0 and 1. Generally, $a \div b = {}^a/_b$ even if $a < b$. This can be a huge cognitive shift for students: that a fraction can represent a quotient. Specifically, $2 ÷ 5$ people results in a share of $^2/_5$ of a dollar per person.

4. **Deliver the $3 ÷ 5 string, p. 107**

Use the discussion on p. 107 to inform your delivery of the string. After the participants answer each question in the string, compare it to the others in the string. Spend time developing the idea that we can build fraction equivalence based on ratio equivalence: if $3 is shared by 5 people, is that equivalent to $6 shared by 10 people, $\frac{3}{5} = \frac{6}{10}$?

Addition with money

- **Deliver the combined ½ + ¼ string in this guide**
- **Discuss the possible denominators using a money model**
- **Display and discuss the strings, p. 131**

1. **Deliver the combined ½ + ¼ string in this guide**
   Ask participants to use money to add the fractions.
   Use the example on p. 129-130 to guide your delivery.
   Ask the participants to use money to explain how they simplify any fractions. See the $\frac{6}{10} = \frac{3}{5}$ discussion on p. 130.
   Bring out that the participants can use splitting or give and take strategies for the mixed number problems. Model both using money, compare, and discuss.

   When might it be advantageous to keep one addend whole? [When one addend is close to a friendly number. For example 99 ¾ + 2 ½. Just tack on ¼ to 99 ¾ to get 100. Then add the remaining 1 ¼.]

   Take note of the ways that the participants use unit fractions to scale up to the other fractions. For example, to find ⅖, a participant might reason that ⅕ of a dollar is 20 cents. Therefore, ⅖ of a dollar is twice that, or 40 cents.

2. **Discuss the possible denominators using a money model**
   Use discussion on p. 131 to guide your conversation.

   What denominators work well with the money model?
   Discuss the relationship between ¼ and $\frac{1}{25}$ and the money model.
   How might students become confused with ¼ and $0.25 and $\frac{1}{25}$?
   How could you help them sort it out? [Encourage participants to help students sort it out by giving them problems like ¼ + $\frac{1}{25}$.]
   What other fractions posses this reciprocal type relationship using the money model? [$\frac{1}{20}$, ⅕, $\frac{1}{50}$, ½]

3. **Display and discuss the strings, p. 131**
   Ask participants to look over the strings and discuss them in their table groups. Ask a couple of groups to share their observations and impressions with the whole group.

FACILITATION TIP

The work in this chapter focuses on finding equivalent fractions. It's all about equivalence. Once students can find equivalent fractions, the operations of addition and subtraction take care of themselves. When adding or subtracting fractions with common denominators, we are free to use many of the whole number addition and subtraction strategies. Therefore, the main task is using equivalence to find common denominators.

FACILITATION TIP

Just like with whole number addition, we use get-to-a-friendly-number, splitting, and give-and-take strategies with fraction addition.

Encourage participants to review their whole number addition posters as needed.

FACILITATION TIP

If your participants have not done much work with whole number subtraction, you may want to lead a few whole number subtraction strings to develop the strategies of removal, finding the difference, and constant difference.

Encourage the participants to justify the strategy they choose based on the numbers in the problem.

Subtraction with money

- **Deliver the combined ¾ – ½ string in this guide**
- **Display and discuss the strings, p. 132**
- **Name the strategy and post it**

1. **Deliver the combined ¾ – ½ string in this guide**

   Ask the participants to use money to subtract the fractions.

   Ask the participants to use money to explain how they simplify any fractions. See the $^6/_{10} = ^3/_5$ discussion on p. 130.

   Bring out that the participants can use a subtraction strategy of removal, difference, or constant difference.

   What about these fractions or their money equivalents, suggests to you that you should use that strategy? [If the fractions are close together, you might find the difference. If the fractions are far apart, you might remove the small one. Regardless, you might shift the distance using the constant difference strategy.]

FACILITATION TIP

When naming the strategy here, we are focusing on the strategy used to manipulate the fractions such that one can add them. The problems in the strings do not have common denominators. The strategy we used to find common denominators was to express them in terms of money so the denominator was the implied 100.

2. **Display and discuss the strings, p. 132**

   Ask the participants to look over the strings and discuss them in their table groups. Ask a couple of groups to share their observations and impressions with the whole group.

3. **Name the strategy and post it**

   Ask the participants to describe the strategy that most of them were using by the end of the string.

   Turn to your partner, and describe what you were doing in addition and subtraction with money strings in order to make it so you could add or subtract. Try to generalize the kinds of things you were doing to make the fractions easier to add or subtract.
   Now, share your generalization with the group.
   What can we call this strategy to refer to this way of manipulating the numbers?

   Post the name and an example problem on large chart paper.

   Which problem in this string would you choose to represent this strategy of using money to find equivalent fractions?

Finding Equivalent Fractions using Money

1 1/4 + 4/5 = $1.25+$0.80
= $2.05
= 2 5/100 = 2 1/20

1/2 − 1/10 = $0.50−$0.10
= $0.40
= 4/10 = 2/5

Addition with a clock model

- **Develop fractional equivalencies with the clock model**
- **Show the Jordan fraction addition video and discuss**
- **Deliver the combined ½ + ⅓ string in this guide**
- **Name the strategy, and post it**

1. **Develop fractional equivalencies with the clock model**
   Use the paragraph on p. 132 to guide this discussion.
   Ask the participants to use a clock and chunks of time to find some equivalent fractions for ½. As participants suggest them, model the equivalencies by writing the fractions and sketching in the chunks on a clock as in Figure 9.9 on p. 133.
   Repeat this for ⅓ (20 minute chunks) and ¼ (15 minute chunks).
   Ask questions:

   What other fractions are handy using a clock model? [⅕, ⅙, ⅒, 1/12, 1/15, 1/20, 1/30, 1/60]
   What chunks of time does each fraction represent?
   ⅕ (12 minute chunks), ⅙ (10 minute chunks), ⅒ (6 minute chunks), 1/12 (5 minute chunks), 1/15 (4 minute chunks), 1/20 (3 minute chunks), 1/30 (2 minute chunks), 1/60 (1 minute chunks)

2. **Show the Jordan fraction addition video, and discuss**
   In this video, Jordan is a sophomore in algebra II. I asked him the questions cold.

   What strategy does Jordan use to add ½ + ⅓?

3. **Deliver the combined ½ + ⅓ string in this guide**

FACILITATION TIP

In the money strings, you state the equivalencies using chunks of money.

6/10 is equivalent to 3/5 using money because 6 dimes out of 10 dimes is equivalent to 3 (20 cent) chunks out of 5 (20 cent) chunks.

Similarly, with the clock model, you use chunks of time.

6/10 is equivalent to 3/5 using a clock model because 6 (6 minute chunks) out of 10 (6 minute chunks) is equivalent to 3 (12 minute chunks) out of 5 (12 minute chunks).

6/10 = 3/5

Explain that you have just done the first problem of the Jordan string, so you will start with the second problem, ⅓ + ¼.

Use the example of p. 133-134 to guide your delivery.

Ask the participants to use chunks of time to explain how they simplify fractions.

Subtraction with a clock model

- Show the Jordan fraction subtraction video
- Deliver the combined ½ – ⅓ string in this guide
- Display and discuss the strings, p. 135
- Name the strategy, and post it

1. **Show the Jordan fraction subtraction video**
   Show the video. Ask the participants to explain Jordan's strategy.

2. **Deliver the combined ½ – ⅓ string in this guide**
   Explain that you have just done the first problem in the Jordan video so you will ask the second problem, ⅚ – ½.
   Draw participant strategies on clocks.
   Encourage removal and difference strategies as discussed on p. 135-136.
   Ask participants to use chunks of time to explain how they simplify fractions.

3. **Display and discuss the strings, p. 135**
   Ask the participants to look over the strings and discuss them in their table groups. Ask a couple of groups to share their observations and impressions with the whole group.

4. **Name the strategy, and post it**
   Ask the participants to describe the strategy that most of them were using by the end of the string.

   > *Turn to your partner, and describe what you were doing every time to find equivalent fractions. Try to generalize the kinds of things you were doing to find common denominators.*
   > *Now, share your generalization with the group.*
   > *What can we call this strategy to refer to this way of manipulating the numbers?*

   Post the name and an example problem on large chart paper.

   > *Which problem in this string would you choose to represent this strategy of using a clock to find equivalent fractions?*

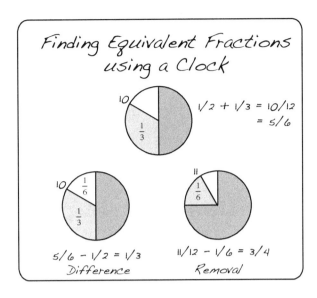

Finding Equivalent Fractions
using a Clock

$1/2 + 1/3 = 10/12$
$= 5/6$

$5/6 - 1/2 = 1/3$
Difference

$11/12 - 1/6 = 3/4$
Removal

Choose Your Model

- **Deliver the ¼ + ⅔ string, p. 137**
- **Invent some money, clock, and either problems**

1. **Deliver the ¼ + ⅔ string, p. 137**
    Ask each problem, share strategies, and discuss which model the
    participants prefer for the numbers in the problem.

    *How does a string like choose your model promote flexibility for
    students?*

2. **Invent some money, clock, and either problems**
    Challenge the participants to write their own problems that are par-
    ticularly suited for the money model, the clock model, and some that
    work well with both models.
    Have each group submit 1 for each type to a whole group poster.
    Have the whole group discuss the problems.

    What are the similarities within each group?

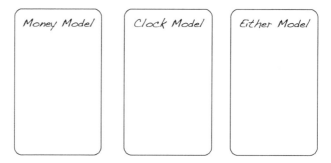

Money Model   Clock Model   Either Model

Choose Your Denominator, Part I

- Deliver the ⅕ + ⅐ string, p. 137
- Discuss the double number line model

1. **Deliver the ⅕ + ⅐ string, p. 137**
   Use the example on p. 137-139 to deliver the string.
   Use double number lines to model strategies.
   Draw the jumps proportionally so that the number lines are lined up and the answers land at the same place.

2. **Discuss the double number line model**

   How does the double number line promote student thinking? [Like the open number line, the array, the clock model, and percent bars, the double number calls for action.]

   Help the participants to see that, as you make the decision of how long to draw the jump for a fraction, the length also suggests how to find the fractional amount of the total. In other words, in order to draw a jump that looks approximately ⅕ of 35, you must approximate dividing 35 into 5 sections. This suggests dividing 35 by 5 to know that the distance traveled is 7. The action of figuring out where to end the jump is the action that suggests how to find the fractional amount.

   Also, help the participants to note that you can find the unit fraction length and then scale up for other fractions. In other words, once you have found that ⅕ of 35 is 7, then ⅗ of 35 is 3 times 7, or 21.

   Also note that, by allowing the participants to find their own course lengths, you encourage them to choose denominators that make sense. The solution is not always to find the lowest common denominator. As long as students can find equivalent fractions with facility, any nice denominator will do.

   Then have students compare their denominators with those of other students. This helps them to continue to refine their choices.

3. **Name the strategy, and post it**

Ask the participants to describe the strategy that most were using by the end of the string.

> *Turn to your partner, and describe what you were doing every time to find equivalent fractions. Try to generalize the kinds of things you were doing to find common denominators.*
> *Now, share your generalization with the group.*
> *What can we call this strategy to refer to this way of manipulating the numbers?*

Post the name and an example problem on large chart paper.

> *Which problem in this string would you choose to represent this using a double number line to find equivalent fractions strategy?*

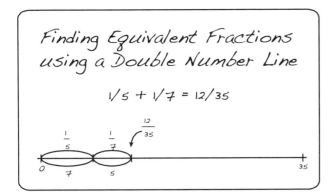

Choose Your Denominator, Part II

- Deliver the ½ + ⅓ + ¼ string, p. 137
- Discuss the rational expression extension, p. 141

1. **Deliver the ½ + ⅓ + ¼ string, p. 137**

Use the example on p. 139-141 to deliver the string.

Use ratio tables to model strategies.

Compare using a double number line and a ratio table to find equivalent fractions. Use the examples on p. 140-141.

2. **Discuss the rational expression extension, p. 141**

Solve the example on p. 141-142.

> *How would students' prior experience with multiplication and division in ratio tables influence their work with rational expressions in ratio tables?*

Give participants rational expressions to add and subtract in ratio tables. Compare strategies.

Comparing Strategies

Give participants the problems on p. 142.

Circulate and observe.

Ask a couple of participants to display their strategy for each problem. Discuss. Focus the discussion on what it is about the numbers that influences their strategy choice.

As Close As It Gets

Display the fraction questions on p. 143, one at a time.

Ask participants to quietly think about which answer choice is as close as they can get to the correct answer.

If time permits, ask partners to discuss their reasoning.

Ask a couple of participants to share their reasoning with the group. Remember:

• Show each problem, one at a time.

• Discuss each before moving to the next problem.

• Don't just round. That answer may not be the closest.

Relational Thinking

Display the fraction questions on p. 144, one at a time.

Ask participants to quietly think about the number that goes in the blank without computing. Instead suggest that they use relational thinking.

> *Can you use relational thinking—how the numbers are related with that equal sign—to fill in the blanks? Don't compute! Don't "solve the equation", but rather use the relationships to find the missing number.*

Have partners discuss their reasoning and then share with the whole group.

Discuss the true/false questions.

Notes:

Fraction Addition & Subtraction
Participant Assignments

1. **Read Chapter 1.**
   Are you a "Kim" or a "Dana"? Describe your experience of learning to compute. What parts of numeracy on p. 3 played a role in your experience? How do you think with numbers now? How do you solve ½ — ⅓?

2. **Read Chapter 8 p. 105-112.**
   How do you find equivalent fractions? How does the quotient meaning of fractions influence the way that you can discuss equivalent fractions? What does it mean that, once students can find equivalent fractions, addition and subtraction of fractions take care of themselves?

3. **Read Chapter 9 p. 129-144.**
   Ask several people, including colleagues and students, "What is ½ + ⅓?" and "What is ⅕ + ½₀?" Describe their responses.

4. **Deliver the Fractions are Quotient strings on p. 107.**

5. **Deliver the Fraction Addition with Money strings, p. 131.**

6. **Deliver the Fraction Subtraction with Money strings, p. 132.**

7. **Deliver Fraction Addition on a Clock strings, p. 134.**

8. **Deliver Fraction Subtraction on a Clock strings, p. 135.**

9. **Deliver Double Number Line/Ratio Table strings, p. 137.**

10. **Intersperse the strings with As Close As It Gets and Relational Thinking problems.**

11. **Look for opportunities to use the strategies while doing the math at hand.**
    Force yourself to slow down and think about the numbers. Invite the participants to share moments of clarity when they apply numeracy or reasoning instead of rote memorization.

12. **Mixed Numbers**
    When adding or subtracting mixed numbers, should you always convert to improper fractions first? Why or why not? Provide examples to support your answer. What is it about the numbers that justifies your thinking?

CHAPTER 6 *six* 6

Fractions: Multiplication & Division

Fractions

At a Glance

Materials

Blank paper, several sheets per participant

Large chart paper

Chart markers

Document camera

Projector

Speakers

Big Ideas

It's all about equivalence
Interpretations of rational numbers:
    Part-whole comparison, measurement, operator, quotient, ratio
Relations on relations

Models

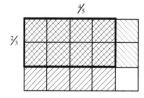

÷ 2	× 3	
Cups of Cheese	⅖	⅕	⅗
Part of Pizza	⅔	⅓	1

÷ 2   × 3

Strategies

Product of unit fractions
Scaling up
Trading places
Doubling/halving
Using common denominators to divide
Constant ratio

Preparation

- Read Chapter 1.
- Read Chapter 8, p. 112-115, 120-124.
- Read Chapter 10, p. 156-169.
- Practice sketching models for each of the strings.
- Ask several people to make up a realistic fraction division problem in context and note their responses. Most, if not all, will suggest fraction multiplication problems.
- Look for real opportunities in your life to multiply and divide fractions using the strategies in this chapter. Be prepared to share your experiences.
- Work the Comparing Strategies problems on p. 165 on your own.

Multiplication & Division

At a Glance

Product of Unit Fractions

$$\frac{1}{3} \cdot \frac{1}{2}$$
$$\frac{1}{2} \cdot \frac{1}{4}$$
$$\frac{1}{3} \cdot \frac{1}{4}$$

p. 156

Scaling Up

$$\frac{1}{3} \cdot \frac{1}{5}$$
$$\frac{2}{3} \cdot \frac{1}{5}$$
$$\frac{2}{3} \cdot \frac{4}{5}$$
$$\frac{1}{4} \cdot \frac{1}{2}$$
$$\frac{5}{4} \cdot \frac{1}{2}$$
$$\frac{5}{4} \cdot \frac{3}{2}$$

p. 157

Trading Places

$$\frac{3}{5} \cdot \frac{4}{7}$$
$$\frac{4}{5} \cdot \frac{3}{7}$$
$$\frac{3}{4} \cdot \frac{2}{5}$$
$$\frac{3}{7} \cdot \frac{2}{4}$$

p. 158

Doubling/Halving

$$6 \cdot 8$$
$$12 \cdot 4$$
$$24 \cdot 1\frac{1}{2}$$
$$\frac{3}{4} \cdot 48$$
$$12 \cdot 3$$
$$20 \cdot 1\frac{1}{2}$$
$$\frac{3}{4} \cdot 12$$

p. 160

Whole Number Divided by a Fraction

$$2 \div \frac{1}{3}$$
$$4 \div \frac{1}{3}$$
$$3 \div \frac{1}{4}$$
$$6 \div \frac{1}{4}$$
$$6 \div \frac{1}{3}$$
$$6 \div \frac{2}{3}$$
$$2 \div \frac{1}{5}$$
$$2 \div \frac{2}{5}$$

p. 161

Fractions Divided by Fractions

$$6 \div 3 = 2$$
$$\frac{5}{6} \div \frac{1}{6}$$
$$\frac{5}{8} \div \frac{1}{8}$$
$$\frac{2}{3} \div \frac{1}{3}$$
$$\frac{3}{2} \div \frac{1}{2}$$
$$\frac{3}{2} \div \frac{1}{4}$$
$$3\frac{1}{2} \div \frac{1}{4}$$
$$\frac{2}{3} \div \frac{1}{3}$$

p. 161

Constant Ratio

$$2 \div \frac{1}{2}$$
$$2 \div \frac{1}{3}$$
$$1 \div \frac{1}{5}$$
$$1 \div \frac{2}{5}$$
$$2 \div \frac{2}{5}$$
$$2 \div \frac{1}{5}$$
$$4 \div \frac{2}{3}$$
$$4 \div \frac{1}{3}$$

p. 163

Constant Ratio

$$\frac{1}{5} \div \frac{1}{3}$$
$$\frac{2}{5} \div \frac{2}{3}$$
$$\frac{1}{4} \div \frac{1}{5}$$
$$\frac{3}{4} \div \frac{3}{5}$$
$$\frac{1}{5} \div \frac{1}{3}$$
$$\frac{4}{5} \div \frac{4}{3}$$
$$\frac{3}{5} \div \frac{3}{4}$$

p. 163

Comparing Strategies

p. 164

As Close As It Gets

p. 166

Relational Thinking

p. 168

Workouts

Fractions: Multiplication & Division

Detailed Plan

Product of Unit Fractions

- Introduce the array model for fraction multiplication, p. 156
- Deliver the ⅓ · ½ string, p. 156
- Name the strategy, and post it
- Emphasize the denominators/dimensions relationship

FACILITATION TIP

The arrays modeling fraction multiplication problems should be in proportion such that the grid lines form squares. This makes rotating the inner array possible for developing the commutative property trading places strategy later. Draw the arrays in proportion now to be consistent.

Square grid:

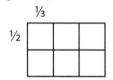

non-square grid:

1. **Introduce the array model for fraction multiplication, p. 156**
   Just as we used arrays to model multiplication for whole numbers, we can use arrays to model multiplication of fractions.

2. **Deliver the ⅓ · ½ string, p. 156**
   Use the example of the brownie pan on p. 156 to deliver the string.

3. **Name the strategy, and post it**
   Ask participants to describe the strategy that most of them were using by the end of the string.

   Turn to your partner, and describe what you were doing every time. Try to generalize the kinds of things you were doing.
   Now, share your generalization with the group.
   What can we call this strategy to refer to this way of manipulating the numbers?

   Post the name and an example problem on large chart paper.

   Which problem in this string would you choose to represent this product of unit fractions strategy?

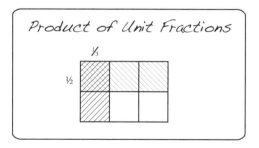

4. **Emphasize the denominators/dimensions relationship**
Ask participants to generalize the relationships discussed on p. 157.

> *What are the relationships between the denominators when finding the product of unit fractions? [The denominators of the fractions determine the dimensions of the array. The dimensions of the array determine the size of piece, or, in other words, the denominator of the product. So, the product of the denominators of the factors is the denominator of the product.]*
>
> *What is the product of 2 unit fractions? [Another unit fraction whose denominator is the product of the unit fractions' denominator.]*

Scaling Up

- Deliver the $\frac{1}{5} \cdot 20$ string, p. 157
- Deliver the $\frac{1}{3} \cdot \frac{1}{5}$ string, p. 157
- Name the strategy, and post it
- Emphasize the inner array/outer array relationship

1. **Deliver the $\frac{1}{5} \cdot 20$ string, p. 157**
Deliver this string quickly emphasizing the scaling up happening from the unit fraction to the rest of the fractions.
Discuss that this kind of string helps to develop the operator meaning of fractions.

> *How might this string influence students when finding $\frac{3}{7}$ of any number? [They might find $\frac{1}{7}$ of the number first and then scale up by 3.]*
>
> *Where else do we find scaling up in the curriculum? How might this influence that work?*

2. **Deliver the 1/3 · 1/5 string, p. 157**
Use the example on p. 157-158 to deliver the string.
Make sure you emphasize the indicated words in the example to bring out the scaling.

3. **Name the strategy, and post it**
Ask the participants to describe the strategy that most of them were using by the end of the string.

> *Turn to your partner, and describe what you were doing every time.*
> *Try to generalize the kinds of things you were doing.*
> *Now, share your generalization with the group.*
> *What can we call this strategy to refer to this way of manipulating*

Sometimes participants are less enthused about fraction multiplication strings because their students "get" fraction multiplication so easily. Gently suggest that, while students do well with fraction multiplication on the days it is taught, students are less clear when to multiply. If they learn fraction multiplication as one more fraction rule, they may mix that rule up with all of the other fraction operation rules.

We want students to understand fraction multiplication, not just what to do.

the numbers?

Post the name and an example problem on large chart paper.

Which problem in this string would you choose to represent this scaling up strategy?

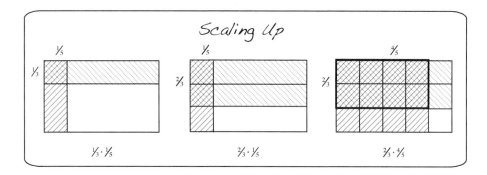

4. **Emphasize the inner array/outer array relationship**
    Use p. 158 to guide your discussion.

    How does scaling up build on the product of unit fractions?
    Where do you see an outer array in our models of fraction multiplication?
    What determines the dimensions of the outer array?
    Where do you see an inner array?
    What determines the dimensions of the inner array?

FACILITATION TIP

The inner array/outer array relationship is an important outcome here. We use it to build the trading places strategy.

Trading Places
-   **Deliver the ³/₅ · ⁴/₇ string, p. 158**
-   **Do the problems in the ⁹/₁₆ · ⁴/₃ and ³/₅ · ⁴/₇ strings, p. 158**
-   **Name the strategy, and post it**

1. **Deliver the ³/₅ · ⁴/₇ string, p. 158**
    As you deliver the string, tell the participants that these problems gives them some practice scaling up to find fraction products. Since the first two products are equivalent, the participants may begin to wonder why. Do the second set of paired problems before you ask participants to investigate.
    Discuss the inner and outer arrays.

    Which problem, 3/4 · 2/5 or 3/7 · 2/4, would you rather solve? Why?

How does this influence the way that you might attach future fraction multiplication problems? [Look to rotate the array so that the numerators switch places. See if this results in fractions that have nice equivalent fractions for the problem.]

2. **Solve the problems in the ⁹⁄₁₆ · ⁴⁄₃ and ³⁄₅ · ⁴⁄₇ strings, p. 158**
    Ask participants to work together to solve the problems in the strings. Have them share their experience.

    What do you think about this strategy?
    What percentage of fraction multiplication problems might have numbers that work well for this strategy? [Since many, if not most, fraction multiplication problems in books are set up to have many opportunities to divide out common factors, this strategy often makes those problems easier to solve.]

3. **Name the strategy, and post it**
    Ask the participants to describe the strategy that most of them were using by the end of the string.

    Turn to your partner, and describe what you were doing every time. Try to generalize the kinds of things you were doing.
    Now, share your generalization with the group.
    What can we call this strategy to refer to this way of manipulating the numbers?
    Post the name and an example problem on large chart paper.

    Which problem in this string would you choose to represent this trading places strategy?

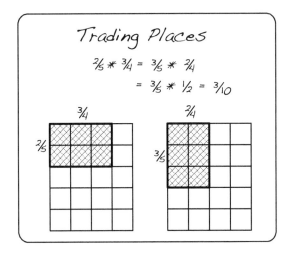

Doubling/Halving

- Deliver the 6 · 8 string on p. 160
- Invent doubling/halving fraction multiplication problems
- Name the strategy, and post it

1. **Deliver the 6 · 8 string on p. 160**

   If your participants have experience with whole number doubling/halving, deliver this string quickly. If not, you may want to do some whole number doubling/halving work with your participants first. Add the problem, 27 · 3 ⅓.

   Discuss the distributive property. When you triple 3 ⅓, you must triple the 3 and the ⅓ and then add those partial products to get 9 + 1 = 10. Have participants model problems on arrays to see this.

   See the doubling/halving section on whole number multiplication to see a full treatment of using the associative property in this way.

2. **Invent doubling/halving fraction multiplication problems**

   Ask groups to work together to invent some fraction multiplication problems for which the doubling/halving strategy works particularly well.

   What about these numbers makes the problems good candidates for doubling/halving?

3. **Name the strategy, and post it**

   Ask the participants to describe the strategy that most of them were using by the end of the string.

   Turn to your partner, and describe what you were doing every time. Try to generalize the kinds of things you were doing.
   Now, share your generalization with the group.
   What could we call this strategy to refer to this way of manipulating the numbers?

   Post the name and an example problem on large chart paper.

   Which problem in this string would you choose to represent this over and under strategy?

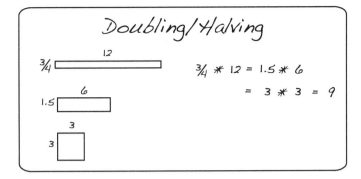

Doubling/Halving

$$\frac{3}{4} * 12 = 1.5 * 6$$
$$= 3 * 3 = 9$$

NOTE

You may not find many textbook problems that work well with the doubling/halving strategy for fraction multiplication. These problems tend to appear in real life more than they do in textbooks.

Common Denominators:
Whole Numbers Divided By Fractions

- Deliver the 2 ÷ ⅓ string, p. 161
- Discuss unit fractions and scaling

1. **Deliver the 2 ÷ ⅓ string, p. 161**
   This string uses the quotative meaning of division.
   Remind the participants that they can consider the quotative meaning of division as the number of the divisors that divide into the dividend.
   When you deliver each problem, state it like this: "How many ⅓s are there in 2?" and write 2 ÷ ⅓.
   Use models like those on p. 161 as you discuss each problem.

2. **Discuss unit fractions and scaling**
   Ask the participants to discuss the connection between the problems where the divisor is a unit fraction and the problems where the divisor is a multiple of that unit fraction.

   If twelve ⅓'s are in 4 (4 ÷ ⅓ = 12), how many ⅔'s are in 4? (4 ÷ ⅔ = ?) [Since ⅔ takes up twice as much of the array as ⅓ does, there must be half as many ⅔'s as ⅓'s.]

FACILITATION TIP

For these common denominator strings to work correctly, the participants should already understand how to find equivalent fractions. These strings do not teach equivalent fractions; they use an already-established sense of equivalency to develop division strategies for fractions.

Work through the addition and subtraction strings to help the participants to construct equivalent fractions.

Common Denominators:
Fractions Divided By Fractions

- Deliver the 6 ÷ 3 string, p. 161
- Deliver the 3 ÷ 1 ½ string, p. 161
- Deliver the 3 ÷ 2 string, p. 161
- **Name the strategy, and post it**

1. **Deliver the 6 ÷ 3 string, p. 161**
   Use p. 162 to guide your delivery.
   Remind the participants of the two meanings of subtraction.
   6 ÷ 3 can be expressed as:
   - "How many 3's in 6?" or as
   - "If you chunk 6 into 3 groups, how many in each group?"
   Help the participants to generalize that five $\frac{1}{a}$ s are in $\frac{5}{a}$.

2. **Deliver the 3 ÷ 1 ½ string, p. 161**
   Use p. 162 to guide your delivery. Bring out the points listed there.
   This string includes mixed numbers.

3. **Deliver the 3 ÷ 2 string, p. 161**
   Use p. 162 to guide your delivery. Bring out the points listed there.
   This string leads to the following generalization:
   $$\frac{a}{b} \div \frac{c}{b} = a \div c$$

   In other words, the number of c/b in a/b is the same as $a \div c$.
   This is true even when c does not divide a evenly and when $a < c$.

4. **Name the strategy, and post it**
   Ask the participants to describe the strategy that most of them were using by the end of the string.

   > *Turn to your partner, and describe what you were doing every time. Try to generalize the kinds of things you were doing.*
   > *Now, share your generalization with the group.*
   > *What can we call this strategy to refer to this way of manipulating the numbers?*

   Post the name and an example problem on large chart paper.

   > *Which problem in this string would you choose to represent this common denominator division strategy?*

> **Dividing with Common Denominators**
>
> $\frac{3}{4} \div \frac{3}{8} = \frac{6}{8} \div \frac{3}{8}$
>
> $= 6 \div 3 = 2$

Notes:

Constant Ratio

- Deliver the 2 ÷ ½ string on p. 163 using a ratio context
- Deliver the ⅕ ÷ ⅓ string on p. 163 using a ratio context
- Deliver the 4 ÷ 3/5 string on p. 163
- Name the strategy, and post it

1. **Deliver the 2 ÷ 1/2 string on p. 163 using a ratio context**

   Set this string in the context of cups of grated cheese needed to make pizzas and parts of a pizza.

   Use the example on p. 163 to guide your delivery. Just as the example suggests, solve the first problem in the ratio table before you ask which equation to write to represent the scenario.

   Make the following points as in the example:
   - we can use ratios to solve division problems and division to solve ratio problems
   - to find the amount of cheese for 1 pizza, you must multiply by the denominator of the divisor.

2. **Deliver the 1/5 ÷ 1/3 string on p. 163 using a ratio context**

   Keep this string in the same context of cups of grated cheese for pizzas. Use p. 164-165 to guide your delivery. Continue to use language about scaling up and down.

   In this string, write equations next to the ratio tables to represent what students did.

$$\frac{2}{5} \div \frac{2}{3} = \left(\frac{2}{5} \div 2\right) \div \left(\frac{2}{3} \div 2\right)$$
$$= \frac{1}{5} \div \frac{1}{3}$$
$$= \frac{1}{5}(3) \div \frac{1}{3}(3)$$
$$= \frac{3}{5} \div 1$$
$$= \frac{3}{5}$$

   Help the participants to make these generalizations:
   - to get to unit fractions, divide by the numerator of the divisor
   - to get to a whole pizza (the divisor = 1), multiply by the denominator of the divisor

   The next string helps participants to put this together in one step.

3. **Deliver the 4 ÷ 3/5 string on p. 163**

   This string gives the participants a chance to answer, "How can I scale the problem so the divisor is 1?"

As you work through the string, help the participants make these generalization:

- to get the divisor to 1, multiply both fractions by the reciprocal of the divisor

    How does this relate to the invert and multiply rule?
    Is this the reason you can invert and multiply? Because it results in the divisor being 1?

When you get to the last problem in the string, $\dfrac{4}{x^2} \div \dfrac{2}{x}$, ask the participants to apply what they have been learning to this rational expression. Encourage them to compare the answer to the solution if they invert and multiply.

Try these problems:

$\dfrac{x}{x^2+x-2} \div \dfrac{x^2}{x-1}$ (This is shown on p. 124)

$\dfrac{x^2+5x+6}{x+2} \div \dfrac{x^2+2x-3}{3x}$

4. **Name the strategy, and post it**

    Ask the participants to describe the strategy that most of them were using by the end of the string.

    Turn to your partner, and describe what you were doing every time.
    Try to generalize the kinds of things you were doing.
    Now, share your generalization with the group.
    What can we call this strategy to refer to this way of manipulating the numbers?

    Post the name and an example problem on large chart paper.

    Which problem in this string would you choose to represent this constant ratio division strategy?

Comparing Strategies

Give participants the problems on p. 165.
Circulate and observe.
Ask a couple of participants to display their strategy for each problem. Discuss. Focus the discussion on what it is about the numbers that influences their strategy choice.

As Close As It Gets

Display the fraction questions on p. 166, one at a time.
Ask participants to quietly think about which answer choice is as close as they can get to the correct answer.
If time permits, ask partners to discuss their reasoning.
Ask a couple of participants to share their reasoning with the group.
Remember:
• Show each problem, one at a time.
• Discuss each before moving to the next problem.
• Don't just round. That answer may not be the closest.

Relational Thinking

Display the fraction questions on p. 168, one at a time.
Ask participants to quietly think about the number that goes in the blank without computing. Instead suggest that they use relational thinking.

> *Can you use relational thinking—how the numbers are related with that equal sign—to fill in the blanks? Don't compute! Don't "solve the equation", but rather use the relationships to find the missing number.*

Have partners discuss their reasoning and then share with the whole group.
Discuss the true/false questions.

Notes:

Division Participant Assignments

1. **Read Chapter 1.**
   Are you a "Kim" or "Dana"? Describe your experience learning to compute. What parts of numeracy on p. 3 played a role in your experience? How do you think with numbers now? How do you do ⅚ ÷ ⅙?

2. **Read Chapter 8, p. 112-115, 120-124 and Chapter 10, p. 156-169.**
   Ask several people, including colleagues and students, "What is a realistic fraction division problem in context?" Describe their responses. How might working with the constant ratio strategy influence their answers?
   Ask several people, including colleagues and students, "Why invert and multiply?" Describe their responses. What is your response?

3. **Common denominators in fraction division.**
   Ask colleagues and students why you might want to find common denominators when dividing fractions. Note their responses.

4. **Deliver the Product of Unit Fractions string, p. 156.**

5. **Deliver the Scaling Up strings, p. 157.**

6. **Deliver the Trading Places strings, p. 158.**

7. **Deliver the Doubling/Halving strings, p. 159.**

8. **Deliver the Quotative Division strings, p. 160-161.**

9. **Deliver the Partitive Division strings, p. 163**

10. **Intersperse the strings with As Close As It Gets and Relational Thinking problems.**

11. **Look for opportunities to use each of the multiplication and division strategies while doing the math at hand.**
    Force yourself to slow down and think about the numbers. Invite students to share moments of clarity when they apply numeracy and/or reasoning instead of rote memorization.

12. **Find fraction multiplication and division problems in your textbook or high stakes test**
    Go on a scavenger hunt. Look for fraction multiplication problems for which the trading places or doubling/halving strategies work well. Are you surprised how many questions turn into easy questions using the trading places strategy? Look for fraction division questions for which the quotative, common denominator strategy works well.

CHAPTER 7 *seven* 7

Decimals: Addition & Subtraction

Decimals

At a Glance

Materials

Blank paper, several sheets per participant

Large chart paper

Chart markers

Document camera

Projector

Speakers

Big Ideas

Money model
Associative property
Friendly, landmark numbers
Difference (distance) versus removal (take away, minus)
Constant difference

Models

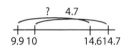

$$\begin{array}{cc} 0.1 & 4.6 \\ \overline{9.9\ 10} & 14.6 \end{array}$$

$$\begin{array}{l} 9.9 + 4.7 \\ +0.1\ -0.1 \\ \hline 10 + 4.6 = 14.6 \end{array}$$

$$\begin{array}{cc} ? & 4.7 \\ \overline{9.9\ 10} & 14.6\,14.7 \end{array}$$

$$\begin{array}{l} 14.6 - 9.9 \\ +0.1\ +0.1 \\ \hline 14.7 - 10 = 4.7 \end{array}$$

Strategies

Get to a friendly number
Partners of 0.1, 0.01
Give and take
Difference (distance)
Removal (take away, minus)
Constant difference

Preparation

- Read Chapter 1.
- Read Chapter 8, p. 105-106.
- Read Chapter 9, p. 125-129.
- Practice sketching models for each of the strings.
- Ask several people how they would find 3.98 + 0.03 and 9.1 − 0.3, and note their responses.
- Look for real opportunities in your life to add and subtract decimals using strategies that maintain magnitude. Be prepared to share your experiences.
- Work the Comparing Strategies problems on p. 128 on your own.

Addition & Subtraction

At a Glance

Get to a Friendly
Number

$14.8 + 0.2$

$14.8 + 0.3$

$7.96 + 0.04$

$7.96 + 0.05$

$3.76 + 1.25$

$0.12 + 5.89$

p. 126

Give & Take

$19.3 + 1.54$

$0.213 + 5.989$

$1.31 + 8.8$

$4.98 + 3.1$

$1.05 + 9.96$

$1.87 + 3.52$

p. 127

Get to Friendly
Number

$19.3 - 0.3$

$19.3 - 0.4$

$2.014 - 0.014$

$2.014 - 0.027$

$13.16 - 0.27$

$7.5 - 3.9$

p. 127

Difference vs Removal

$9.11 - 0.99$

$15.01 - 14.79$

$1,000 - 1.9$

$1,000 - 978.9$

$6.02 - 5.93$

$13.117 - 0.982$

$5.1 - 2.9$

p. 128

Constant Difference

$80.9 - 40$

$80.2 - 39.3$

$59.6 - 10$

$59.4 - 9.8$

$32.6 - 3.7$

$6.5 - 3.9$

$13.26 - 2.78$

p. 128

Constant Difference

$6.5 - 3.9$

$70.2 - 48.7$

$13.05 - 8.98$

$13.117 - 0.982$

$2.0001 - 1.8696$

$5.01 - 2.898$

New

Comparing Strategies

p. 128

As Close As It Gets

p. 143

Relational Thinking

p. 144

Workouts

Decimals: Addition & Subtraction

Detailed Plan

Get to a Friendly Number: Addition

FACILITATION TIP

If your participants have less experience with decimals, you may want to start with a short add a friendly number string:

6.7 + 1

6.7 + 1.4

3.86 + 1

3.86 + 1.2

3.86 + 1.25

0.38 + 0.2

0.38 + 0.23

3.4 + 1.8

This string encourages participants to keep one addend whole, add a friendly number, and then adjust at the end.

- Deliver the 14.8 + 0.2 string, p. 126
- Friendly numbers for decimals
- Name the strategy, and post it

1. **Deliver the 14.8 + 0.2 string, p. 126**
   Deliver the string modeling on an open number line and with splitting.

   Were you more inclined to split the numbers into their place-value parts or add a little to get to a friendly number?

2. **Friendly numbers for decimals**
   Discuss the friendly or landmark numbers for decimals, and compare them to those for whole numbers.

   What are friendly landmark numbers for these decimal problems? How do they compare to those that we used for whole numbers? What do the friendly landmark numbers have to do with money?

3. **Name the strategy, and post it**
   Ask the participants to describe the strategy that most of them were using by the end of the string.

   Turn to your partner, and describe what you were doing every time. Try to generalize the kinds of things you were doing. Now, share your generalization with the group. What can we call this strategy to refer to this way of manipulating the numbers?

   Post the name and an example problem on large chart paper.

   Which problem in this string would you choose to represent this get to a friendly number strategy?

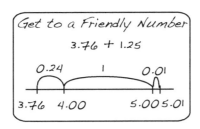

Some participants may use the give and take strategy with problems in the get to a friendly number string. Acknowledge their good work privately, but wait to celebrate it in the group until you do the give and take string work.

Encourage these participants to understand that many of their students may need this precursor work of get to a friendly number before they are ready to try give and take.

Models for the give and take string, p. 127

Give and Take

- Deliver the 2.97 + 1.54 string, p. 127
- Name the strategy and post it

1. **Deliver the 2.97 + 1.54 string, p. 127**
   Use the suggestions on p. 126 to deliver the string.

2. **Name the strategy, and post it**
   Ask the participants to describe the strategy that most of them were using by the end of the string.

   Turn to your partner, and describe what you were doing every time. Try to generalize the kinds of things you were doing.
   Now, share your generalization with the group.
   What can we call this strategy to refer to this way of manipulating the numbers?
   Post the name and an example problem on large chart paper.

   Which problem in this string would you choose to represent this give and take strategy?

The Give and Take Strategy

$$2.97 + 1.54$$
$$+0.03 \quad -0.03$$
$$3.00 + 1.51 = 4.51$$

$$2.97 + 1.54 = 4.51$$

If your participants have not experienced whole number addition work, deliver a whole number get to a friendly number string first. Wait to name and post the strategy until you have done the decimal string.

Get to a Friendly Number: Subtraction

- **Deliver the 19.3 – 0.3 string, p. 127**
- **Clarify that this string prompts "removing"**
- **Name the strategy, and post it**

1. **Deliver the 19.3 – 0.3 string, p. 127**
   Use the example and number lines on p. 127 to deliver the string.

2. **Clarify that this string prompts "removing"**
   This string is structured with paired problems. The first helper problem subtracts easily to a landmark or friendly number. Then the next problem prompts participants to use the helper problem and just remove a little more. Thus, this string prompts participants to use a removal strategy to solve a subtraction problem.

FACILITATION TIP

Since the get to a friendly number strategy is the same for addition and subtraction, you can add it to the poster you made for addition.

3. **Name the strategy, and post it**
   Ask the participants to describe the strategy that most of them were using by the end of the string.

   Turn to your partner, and describe what you were doing every time. Try to generalize the kinds of things you were doing.
   Now, share your generalization with the group.
   What can we call this strategy to refer to this way of manipulating the numbers?

   Post the name and an example problem on large chart paper.

   Which problem in this string would you choose to represent this get to a friendly number strategy?

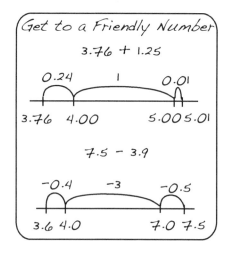

Difference versus Removal

- **Deliver the 9.11 – 0.99 string on p. 128**
- **Discuss the meanings of subtraction**
- **Name the strategy and post it**

1. **Deliver the 9.11 – 0.99 string on p. 128**
   Use the section in this guide on difference versus removal for whole number subtraction to inform your delivery of this string.

2. **Discuss the meanings of subtraction**

   What about the numbers suggests that removal is a good strategy? What about the numbers suggests that finding the difference is a good strategy?
   Where is the answer on the number line when using a removal strategy?
   Where is the answer on the number line when using a difference strategy?

3. **Name the strategy, and post it**
   Ask the participants to describe the strategy that most of them were using by the end of the string.

   Turn to your partner, and describe what you were doing every time. Try to generalize the kinds of things you were doing.
   Now, share your generalization with the group.
   What can we call this strategy to refer to this way of manipulating the numbers?

   Post the name and an example problem on large chart paper.

   Which problem in this string would you choose to represent a removal strategy? A difference strategy?

Difference vs Removal Strategies

$6.02 - 5.93 = 0.09$ $1,000 - 1.9 = 998.1$

If your participants have worked with these strategies with whole numbers, this string should go fairly quickly. Have participants focus on the strategy that makes sense for each problem and on making efficient jumps.

If your participants are new to difference, take more time to develop the contrast between difference and removal. Have participants solve each problem with removal and difference, then compare.

When the numbers are close together, it is easy to find the difference (distance) between them.

When the numbers are relatively far apart, it is easy to remove.

If you have not yet done so, discuss the implications for higher math for the difference meaning of subtraction. See the whole number subtraction section.

Constant Difference

- Deliver the 80.9 — 40 string, p. 128
- Deliver the 5.5 — 3.9 string, new to this guide
- **Name the strategy and post it**

1. **Deliver the 80.9 — 40 string, p. 128**
   This string is constructed with paired problems; the first problem in each pair is easy to solve, and the second problem is equivalent to the first. Allow participants to solve the problems using either removal or difference but model the difference strategy. Keep the number lines aligned and the jumps proportional so that participants can see the equivalent distances shifting up or down the number line.
   The last three problems are given without helper problems. Encourage participants to discuss where to shift the difference to make the problems easier.

2. **Deliver the 5.5 — 3.9 string, new to this guide**
   As you deliver this string, choose 1 or 2 participant strategies to model for each problem. Discuss where to shift the distance to make the problems easier.

3. **Name the strategy, and post it**
   Ask the participants to describe the strategy that most of them were using by the end of the string.

   Turn to your partner, and describe what you were doing every time. Try to generalize the kinds of things you were doing.
   Now, share your generalization with the group.
   What can we call this strategy to refer to this way of manipulating the numbers?

   Post the name and an example problem on large chart paper.

   Which problem in this string would you choose to represent this constant difference strategy?

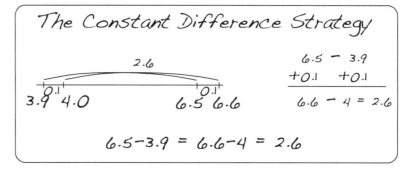

Notes:

Comparing strategies

Give participants the problems on p. 128 to work on.
Circulate, and observe.
Ask a couple of participants to display their strategies for each problem. Discuss. Focus the discussion on what it is about the numbers that influences their strategy choice.

As Close As It Gets

Display the decimal questions on p. 143, one at a time.
Ask participants to quietly think about the answer choice that is as close as they can get to the correct answer.
If time permits, ask partners to discuss their reasoning.
Ask a couple of participants to share their reasoning with the group. Remember:
• Show each problem, one at a time.
• Discuss each before moving to the next problem.
• Avoid just rounding. That answer may not be the closest.

Relational Thinking

Display the decimal questions on p. 144, one at a time.
Ask participants to quietly think about the number that goes in the blank without computing. Instead, suggest that they use relational thinking.

> *Can you use relational thinking* about *how the numbers are related with that equal sign to fill in the blanks? Don't compute. Don't "solve the equation", but, rather, use the relationships to find the missing number.*

Have partners discuss their reasoning and then share with the whole group.
Discuss the true/false questions.

Notes:

Decimal Addition & Subtraction
Participant Assignments

1. **Read Chapter 1.**
   Are you a "Kim" or "Dana"? Describe your experience learning to compute. What parts of numeracy on p. 3 played a role in your experience? How do you think with numbers now? How do you solve $7.02 - 0.97$?

2. **Read Chapter 8 p. 105-106.**
   What are friendly numbers for decimals? How do these relate to money? What does it mean that "students soon learn that they can use their whole number strategies with decimals using place-value understanding to adjust the place value as necessary"? (p. 106)

3. **Read Chapter 9, p. 125-128.**
   Ask several people, including colleagues and students, "What is $10 - 9.2$?" Describe their responses; note especially if they use money.

4. **Deliver the Get to a Friendly Number string, p. 126.**

5. **Deliver the Give and Take string, p. 127.**

6. **Deliver the Subtraction Get to a Friendly Number string, p. 127.**

7. **Deliver the Difference versus Removal string, p. 128.**

8. **Deliver the Constant Difference strings, p. 128 and in this guide.**

9. **Intersperse the strings with As Close As It Gets and Relational Thinking problems.**

10. **Look for opportunities to use the constant difference strategies while doing the math at hand.**
    Force yourself to slow down and think about the numbers. Invite students to share moments of clarity when they apply numeracy or reasoning instead of rote memorization.

11. **Meet or beat the algorithm**
    Do you think you can always meet or beat the algorithm? If yes, invent subtraction problems for which you think you would meet the algorithm. If not, invent problems for which you think the algorithm is the most efficient strategy. Describe the numbers in the problems. Why do you think the algorithm works well for the problems? What kinds of subtraction problems do you think we could agree should be done with technology?

CHAPTER 8 *eight* 8

Decimals: Multiplication & Division

Decimals

At a Glance

Materials

Blank paper, several sheets per participant

Large chart paper

Chart markers

Document camera

Projector

Speakers

Big Ideas

Multiplying by one-tenth and one-hundredth
Associative property
Distributive property
Divide by multiplying
Use whole number strategies and adjust for place-value

Models

1		?
2.4		7.2

$$\frac{56}{0.7} = \frac{560}{7} = 80$$

(diagram: 2.4 over ? with 7.2)

Strategies

Chunking (partial products, partial quotients)
Larger and fewer chunks
Doubling/halving
5 is half of 10, ½ = 0.5
Over and under
Constant ratio
Using whole numbers

Preparation

- Read Chapter 1.
- Read Chapter 8, p. 105-106, 120.
- Read Chapter 10, p. 145-156.
- Practice sketching models for each of the strings.
- Ask several people how they would find $0.25 \cdot 36$ and $42 \div 4$, and note their responses.
- Look for real opportunities in your life to multiply and divide decimals in chunks using strategies that maintain magnitude. Be prepared to share your experiences.
- Work the Comparing Strategies problems on p. 155 on your own.

Multiplication & Division

At a Glance

The Power of a Tenth	The Power of a Tenth	Chunking: The Distributive Property	Multiplication: Over & Under
$8 \cdot 0.1$	$12 \cdot 3$	$1.8 \cdot 2$	$3.4 \cdot 1.1$
$8 \cdot 0.3$	$1.2 \cdot 3$	$1.8 \cdot 0.2$	$3.4 \cdot 0.9$
$8 \cdot 0.05$	$12 \cdot 0.3$	$1.8 \cdot 4$	$0.51 \cdot 4.2$
$8 \cdot 0.15$	$0.12 \cdot 3$	$1.8 \cdot 4.2$	$0.49 \cdot 4.2$
$8 \cdot 0.35$	$3.2 \cdot 2$	$2.3 \cdot 2$	$10.1 \cdot 7.4$
$3 \cdot 0.1$	$32 \cdot 0.2$	$2.3 \cdot 0.2$	$9.9 \cdot 7.4$
$3 \cdot 0.2$	$32 \cdot 0.02$	$2.3 \cdot 1.2$	$99.9 \cdot 12.4$
$3 \cdot 0.05$	$0.32 \cdot 2$	$1.2 \cdot 1.6$	
$3 \cdot 0.06$	$6.1 \cdot 2$		
$3 \cdot 0.26$	$61 \cdot 0.2$		
p. 146	**p. 146**	**p. 147**	**p. 147**

Doubling/Halving	Division	Division: Over & Under	Constant Ratio
$0.51 \cdot 4.2$	$2.5 \div 2.5$	$160 \div 4$	$56/7$
$1.02 \cdot 2.1$	$5 \div 2.5$	$164 \div 4$	$5.6/0.7$
$1.5 \cdot 1.8$	$7.5 \div 2.5$	$162 \div 4$	$56/0.7$
$3 \cdot 0.9$	$0.75 \div 0.75$	$161 \div 4$	$5.6/7$
$1.6 \cdot 3.5$	$3 \div 0.75$	$160.5 \div 4$	$0.56/7$
$2.5 \cdot 3.2$	$3.75 \div 0.75$	$163 \div 4$	$0.56/0.7$
$8.4 \cdot 3.5$	$4.5 \div 0.75$	$166 \div 4$	$56/0.07$
			$138/12$
p. 149	**p. 150**	**p. 151**	**p. 153**

Comparing Strategies	As Close As It Gets	Relational Thinking
p. 102	**p. 102**	**p. 103**

Workouts

Decimals: Multiplication & Division

Detailed Plan

The Power of a Tenth

FACILITATION TIP

Through this entire section, continually seek for different strategies. Model the thinking. Ask participants if money thinking could be helpful. Draw repeated addition on a number line. Use arrays. Use ratio tables. Compare. It's not about which one is right or better; It's about bringing them all together and having the depth of understanding. We want to be able to choose the representation that works well because we have them all to choose from.

- Deliver the 8 · 0.1 string, p. 146
- Deliver the 12 · 3 string, p. 146
- Name the strategy, and post it

1. **Deliver the 8 · 0.1 string, p. 146**
   Deliver the string, modeling with arrays and ratio tables. If the participants do not suggest the following, offer them yourself:

   How do you find 8 times 0.1? How do you reason about it?

If a participants says:	Model and restate:
I think of 8 times one-tenth. That's eight-tenths.	$\frac{1}{10}$ $8 \cdot \frac{1}{10} = \frac{8}{10} = 0.8$ *So, you know that 0.1 is equivalent to $\frac{1}{10}$. I will represent your strategy in an array that is 8 by one-tenth. Eight times $\frac{1}{10}$ is eight tenths, $\frac{8}{10} = 0.8$.*
I think of 8 dimes: 80 cents.	0.1 $8 \cdot 0.1 = 0.8$ *So, 8 times \$0.10 is \$0.80. So I could draw 8 dimes, or I can just relabel the array as 8 by 0.10.*

If a participants says:	Model and restate:
I think of 10% of 8 or 0.80.	10% of 8 is 0.8. *You are using the relationship between percents and decimals. I'll write that in a sentence.*
I know 8 times 1 is 8, so 8 times ⅒ has to be ⅒ of that: ⅒ of 8 is 0.8.	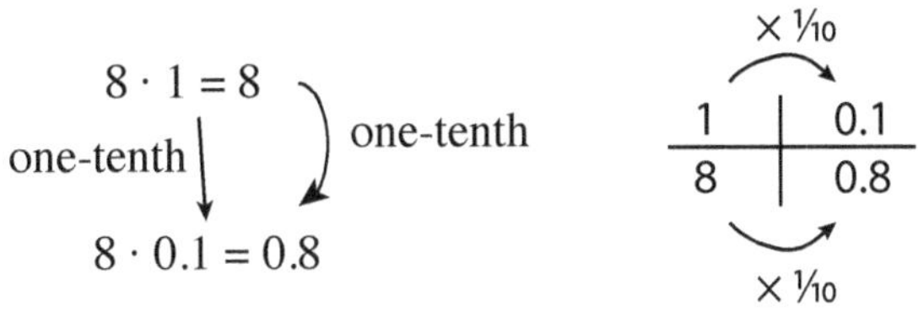 $$8 \cdot 1 = 8$$ one-tenth $\quad$ one-tenth $$8 \cdot 0.1 = 0.8$$ $\times \frac{1}{10}$ $\begin{array}{c\|c} 1 & 0.1 \\ \hline 8 & 0.8 \end{array}$ $\times \frac{1}{10}$ *I can model that in a ratio table. You start with one 8, and then find ⅒ of it.*

What is 8 · 0.3? How do you think about 8 times 0.3?

If a participants says:	Model and restate:
I know that 8 dimes is 80 cents, so 3 times that is 240 cents or $2.40: 2.4.	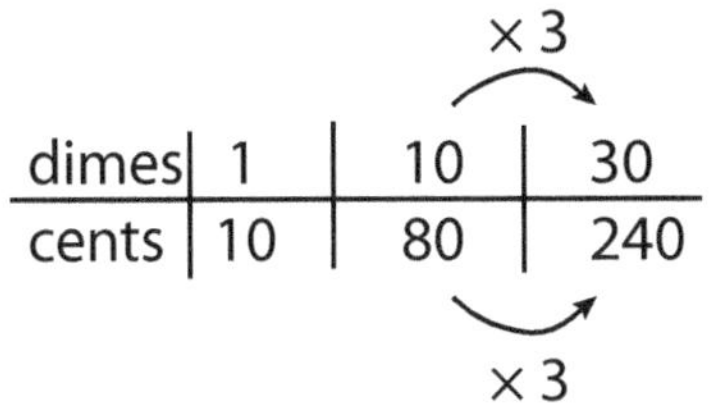 $\times 3$ $\begin{array}{c\|c\|c\|c} \text{dimes} & 1 & 10 & 30 \\ \hline \text{cents} & 10 & 80 & 240 \end{array}$ $\times 3$ *You know, there is 10 cents in a dime, and 8 dimes is 80 cents. Then you find 3 times 80 cents to get 240 cents. That's $2.40 or 8 times 0.3 is 2.4.*
I know 8 times 3 is 24. Then ⅒ of 24 is 2.4.	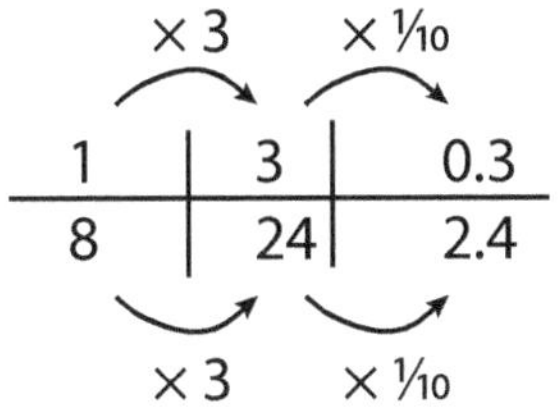 $\times 3 \qquad \times \frac{1}{10}$ $\begin{array}{c\|c\|c} 1 & 3 & 0.3 \\ \hline 8 & 24 & 2.4 \end{array}$ $\times 3 \qquad \times \frac{1}{10}$ *I will model that in a ratio table. You start by finding 8 times 3. Then you find ⅒ of 24.*
I think of 10% of 8. That's 0.80.	10% of 8 is 0.8.

What is 8 · 0.05? How do you think about 8 times 0.05?

FACILITATION TIP

When participants say, "I just move the decimal," encourage them to reason about why that works. Help connect multiplication by 1/10 where the product is.

Also, help participants to see that this string is designed to help students to make the place value connections by comparing their results of fraction multiplication with the results of money multiplication. In other words, teachers will come at the string with prior knowledge. Even if students do not have this prior knowledge, the string helps to construct the relationships.

<table>
<tr><td colspan="2">

FACILITATION TIP

There are two important ideas from whole number multiplication.

You can multiply by 10 and then double and triple up.

23×30 can be found

$23 \times 10 = 230$

$23 \times 20 = 460$

$23 \times 30 = 690$

Using the associative property,

$23 \times 30 =$

$(23 \times 3) \times 10$

$69 \times 10 = 690$

Similarly, these ideas work with decimal multiplication:

You can multiply by 0.1, and then double and triple up.

23×0.3 is

$23 \times 0.1 = 2.3$

$23 \times 0.2 = 4.6$

$23 \times 0.3 = 6.9$

Or

$23 \times 0.3 =$

$(23 \times 3) \times 0.1$

$69 \times 0.1 = 6.9$

</td></tr>
</table>

If a participants says:	Model and restate:
I know that 8 nickels is 40 cents; so it's 0.4.	$\times 8$ nickels $\mid$ 1 $\mid$ 10 cents $\mid$ 5 $\mid$ 40 $\times 8$ You know there is 5 cents in a nickel. And 8 nickels is 40 cents.
Well, we had 8 times $0.1 = 0.8$ already. So, since 0.05 is half of 0.1, then the answer is half of 0.8, or 0.4.	0.1 $\quad$ 0.5 $8 \mid \quad 8 \cdot \frac{1}{10} = 0.8 \quad 8 \mid \quad \frac{1}{2} \cdot 0.8 = 0.4$ $\times \frac{1}{2}$ 1 $\mid$ 0.1 $\mid$ 0.05 8 $\mid$ 0.8 $\mid$ 0.4 $\times \frac{1}{2}$ So, if we cut our previous array in half, we have a 0.5 by 8, and half of the area of 0.8 is 0.4. I can also use our previous ratio table.
If I ignore the 0.05, and multiply 8 times 5, that's 40. Then, since 0.05 is $\frac{1}{100}$ of 5, then the answer is $\frac{1}{100}$ of 40 or 0.4.	$\times 5 \quad \times 0.01$ 1 $\mid$ 5 $\mid$ 0.05 8 $\mid$ 40 $\mid$ 0.4 $\times 5 \quad \times 0.01$ I'll model that in a ratio table. You started with 8, you multiplied by 5, and then you found $\frac{1}{100}$ of that.

Continue the string using arrays and ratio tables to model combining the partial products.

$$8 \cdot 0.15 = 1.2$$

2. **Deliver the 12 · 3 string, p. 146**
   This string is designed to help participants to construct the relationship that you can multiply the whole numbers first and then consider
   the place value shift. Work hard to maintain the language about magnitude and the reason the place value shifts. Encourage participants
   to develop good language: multiplying a number by $\frac{1}{10}$ means that
   the product is $\frac{1}{10}$ of the number.
   These have equivalent results:
   $$\tfrac{1}{10} \cdot n = 0.1 \cdot n$$

   What happens to numbers when we multiply them by 10?
   What happens to numbers when we multiply them by $\frac{1}{10}$; when we
   find $\frac{1}{10}$ of the number?

3. **Name the strategy, and post it.**
   Ask participants to describe the strategy that most of them were using by the end of the string.

   Turn to your partner, and describe what you were doing every time.
   Try to generalize the kinds of things you were doing.
   Now, share your generalization with the group.
   What can we call this strategy to refer to this way of manipulating
   the numbers?
   Post the name and an example problem on large chart paper.

   Which problem in this string would you choose to represent this get
   to a friendly number strategy?

Chunking: The Distributive Property

- Deliver the 1.8 · 2 string, p. 147
- Display and discuss the 3 · 0.1 string, p. 147
- Display and discuss the 16 · 0.5 string, p. 147
- Name the strategy, and post it

1. **Deliver the 1.8 · 2 string, p. 147**
   Use the suggestions and arrays on p. 147 to deliver the string.

2. **Display and discuss the 3 · 0.1 string, p. 147**
   Display the string.
   Ask participants to work together to draw arrays and fill in ratio tables to model each of the problems.
   Ask participants to discuss which model they like best for the string.

3. **Display and discuss the 16 · 0.5 string, p. 147**
   Display the string.
   Talk through the problems having participants discuss the relationships between them. Use the discussion on p. 148 to help.

4. **Name the strategy, and post it.**
   Ask participants to describe the strategy that most of them were using by the end of the string.

   Turn to your partner, and describe what you were doing every time.
   Try to generalize what kinds of things you were doing.
   Now, share your generalization with the group.
   What could we call this strategy to refer to this way of manipulating the numbers?

   Post the name and an example problem on large chart paper.

   Which problem in this string would you choose to represent this chunking strategy?

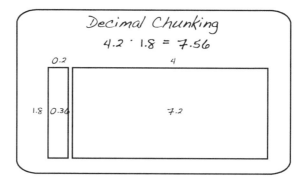

Over & Under: Multiplication

- **Deliver the 3.4 · 1.1 string, p. 148**
- **Deliver the 4.6 · 0.5 string, p. 148**
- **Name the strategy, and post it**
- **Discuss the Sieve of Pam Harris**

1. **Deliver the 3.4 · 1.1 string, p. 148**
   Use ratio tables to model strategies.
   This string is structured with paired problems. One is a little over a landmark multiple, and the other is a little under.
   By the end of the string, participants are multiplying 2 and 3-digit numbers. Ask participants to look over the problems.

   What kinds of numbers are in these problems?
   What relationships did you use to solve the problems?

2. **Deliver the 4.6 · 0.5 string, p. 148**
   This string uses the friendly chunks of halves and quarters. Model strategies in ratio tables. See p. 148 for discussion.

3. **Name the strategy, and post it.**
   Ask participants to describe the strategy that most of them were using by the end of the string.

   Turn to your partner, and describe what you were doing every time.
   Try to generalize the kinds of things you were doing.
   Now, share your generalization with the group.
   What can we call this strategy to refer to this way of manipulating the numbers?

   Post the name and an example problem on large chart paper.

   Which problem in this string would you choose to represent this over and under strategy?

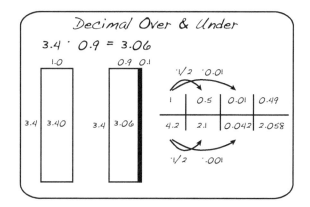

FACILITATION TIP

When using the over strategy, you often subtract a little bit from a friendly number. Encourage participants to think and reason through the subtraction. Draw number lines, and remind participants of the constant difference subtraction strategy.

If your participants have had little or no experience with whole number doubling and halving, consider working through some whole number doubling/ halving strings before delivering this string. Remember, it's about building mental relationships, not about memorizing strategies.

4. Discuss the Sieve of Pam Harris

This is a tongue in cheek reference to the Sieve of Eratosthenes, where you find the prime numbers up to a certain number by process of elimination.

In the Sieve of Pam Harris, you find those numbers that are truly not friendly to multiply. To do this, look at all 2-digit by 2-digit multiplication problems, and eliminate those numbers that are friendly.

Ask participants to identify or characterize some 2-digit numbers that they now know are relatively easy to multiply by.

Now that we have all of these powerful strategies at our finger tips, what numbers are easy to multiply by? Why?

- the decades (multiples of 10) (the power of ten or a tenth)
- near decades (18, 19, 21, 22, 28, 29, 31, 32, etc.) (over and under)
- quarters (25, 75) (use fractions)
- near quarters (24, 26, 74, 76) (use fractions, over and under)
- 5's (multiples of 5) (five is half of 10)
- doubles (44, 66, 84) (double)

What numbers are left? [17, 27, 34, 36, 37, 46, 47, 57, 64, 67, 77, 86, 87, 94, 96, 97]

What could you do when faced with 1 of these unfriendly numbers? [Look at the other factor!]

The worst case scenario is a problem where both factors are ugly, for example 34 · 67 or any of its variations: 3.4 · 67, 0.34 · 6.7, 34 · 0.67, ... What can you do here? [You can use the distributive property and chunk the numbers into parts, about as efficient as using the algorithm, but maintaining magnitude.]

End this discussion by challenging participants to consider the mathematical power and confidence that students gain by constructing the relationships that make all of these mental strategies possible.

Doubling/Halving

- Deliver the 0.51 · 4.2 string on p. 149
- Name the strategy, and post it
- The Sieve of Pam Harris continued

1. Deliver the 0.51 · 4.2 string on p. 149

Use the discussion on p. 149 to inform your delivery of this string. Use arrays to model the problems.

2. Name the strategy, and post it.

Ask participants to describe the strategy that most of them were using by the end of the string.

> *Turn to your partner, and describe what you were doing every time. Try to generalize the kinds of things you were doing.*
> *Now, share your generalization with the group.*
> *What can we call this strategy to refer to this way of manipulating the numbers?*

Post the name and an example problem on large chart paper.

> *Which problem in this string would you choose to represent this doubling/halving strategy?*

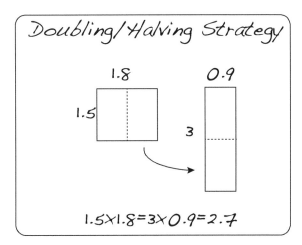

3. The Sieve of Pam Harris continued

Ask participants what factors they might add to the list of friendly factors now that they have added doubling/halving as a decimal multiplication strategy.

> *Now we have this doubling/halving strategy for multiplying decimals, let's look back at our Sieve of Pam Harris list of ugly numbers. Are there any numbers that we can take off of the list? [36, 46, 64 and 96 all halve to very nice numbers]*
> *Let's look at the list again. How many ugly numbers are left? What are they? [12: 17, 27, 34, 37, 47, 57, 67, 77, 86, 87, 94, 97]*

Chunking: Division

- Deliver the 2.5 ÷ 2.5 string, p. 150
- Display and discuss the 1.2 ÷ 1.2 and 2 ÷ 0.02 strings, p. 150
- Display and discuss the string, p. 150

THE SIEVE OF PAM HARRIS

You can argue with my list of ugly numbers. Maybe there is a number on my list that you find particularly friendly. Maybe one of my friendlies is on your ugly list. The point is that the list of numbers for which we cannot find a fabulous strategy is rather smaller than we might have originally thought. Most of the time, we can beat the algorithm. About 12 out of 100 times, we will use about as many steps as in the algorithm. When the numbers get even uglier, I say, pull out a calculator.

FACILITATION TIP

If your participants have had little or no experience with whole number division strategies, consider working through some whole number chunking strings. See the whole number division section for ideas about introducing division on open arrays.

- **Name the strategy, and post it**

1. **Deliver the 2.5 ÷ 2.5 string, p. 150**
   Use the discussion on p. 150 to inform your delivery of this string. Use arrays to model the problems.

2. **Display and discuss the 1.2 ÷ 1.2 and 2 ÷ 0.02 strings, p. 150**
   Use the discussion on p. 149 to inform your discussion of these strings.

3. **Name the strategy, and post it.**
   Ask participants to describe the strategy that most of them were using by the end of the string.

   Turn to your partner, and describe what you were doing every time. Try to generalize the kinds of things you were doing.
   Now, share your generalization with the group.
   What can we call this strategy to refer to this way of manipulating the numbers?

   Post the name and an example problem on large chart paper.

   Which problem in this string would you choose to represent this chunking division strategy?

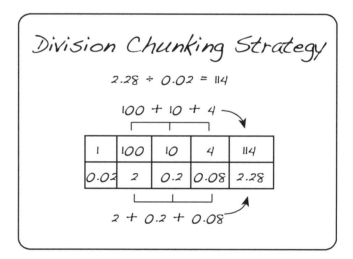

Over and Under: Division

- **Deliver the 160 ÷ 4 string, p. 151**
- **Deliver the 32 ÷ 8 string, p. 151**
- **Name the strategy, and post it**

1. **Deliver the 160 ÷ 4 string, p. 151**
   Use the arrays and discussion on p. 151-152 to guide your delivery of this string. Take your time with these problems discussing the resulting areas.

   Sometimes, participants want to draw a pseudo array, such as the following. If you do have these remaining pieces, you have a remainder as shown.

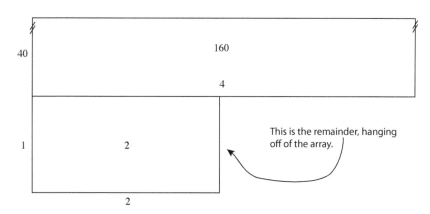

   If you want an exact answer, then the resulting array must be a rectangle. It can't have any left-over remaining pieces. So, the dimensions are 0.5 by 4 to get the area of 2 as shown.

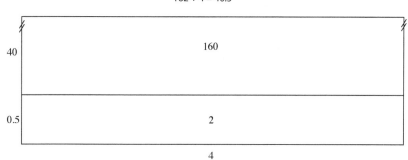

   This shows an array, with no remainder hanging off.

2. **Deliver the 32 ÷ 8 string, p. 151**
   Use the discussion on p. 152-153 as you deliver the string. Model the problems on open arrays.

3. **Name the strategy, and post it.**
   Ask participants to describe the strategy that most of them were using by the end of the string.

Turn to your partner, and describe what you were doing every time.
Try to generalize the kinds of things you were doing.
Now, share your generalization with the group.
What can we call this strategy to refer to this way of manipulating the numbers?

Post the name and an example problem on large chart paper.

Which problem in this string would you choose to represent this over and under division strategy?

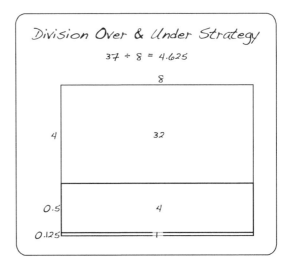

Constant Ratio: Division

- Deliver the 56 ÷ 7 string, p. 153
- Discuss "moving the decimal" in the long division algorithm
- Display and discuss the 164 ÷ 8 and 220 ÷ 22 strings, p. 153
- Name the strategy and post it

1. **Deliver the 56 ÷ 7 string, p. 153**
   The big idea for these strings is that finding equivalent fractions allows us to use whole number division strategies to solve decimal division problems.
   Use the example on p. 154 to inform your delivery of this string.

2. **Discuss "moving the decimal" in the long division algorithm**
   Use the example on p. 154 to discuss "moving the decimal" in the long division algorithm.

   What does this string have to do with "moving the decimal" in the long division algorithm?

3. **Display and discuss the 164 ÷ 8 and 220 ÷ 22 strings, p. 153**
   Have participants discuss how the strings are designed.

   > *Of all of the problems in the string, which do you prefer to solve?*
   > *Which problems would you solve next and why?*
   > *Which problems have a quotient greater than 1? Less than 1?*

4. **Name the strategy, and post it.**
   Ask participants to describe the strategy that most of them were using by the end of the string.

   > *Turn to your partner, and describe what you were doing every time.*
   > *Try to generalize the kinds of things you were doing.*
   > *Now, share your generalization with the group.*
   > *What can we call this strategy to refer to this way of manipulating the numbers?*

   Post the name and an example problem on large chart paper.

   > *Which problem in this string would you choose to represent this constant ratio division strategy?*

Constant Ratio Strategy

$$56 \div 0.07 = 80$$

$$56 \div 0.07 = 56/0.07 = 560/7 = 80$$

Comparing Strategies

Give participants the problems on p. 155 to work on.
Circulate and observe.
Ask a couple of participants to display their strategy for each problem. Discuss. Focus the discussion on what it is about the numbers that influences their strategy choice.

As Close As It Gets

Display the decimal questions on p. 166, one at a time.
Ask participants to quietly think about which answer choice is as close as they can get to the correct answer.
If time permits, ask partners to discuss their reasoning.
Ask a couple of participants to share their reasoning with the group.
Remember:
• Show each problem, one at a time.
• Discuss each before moving to the next problem.
• Don't just round. That answer may not be the closest.

Relational Thinking

Display the decimal questions on p. 168, one at a time.
Ask participants to quietly think about the number that goes in the blank without computing. Instead suggest that they use relational thinking.

> *Can you use relational thinking—how the numbers are related with that equal sign—to fill in the blanks? Don't compute! Don't "solve the equation", but rather use the relationships to find the missing number.*

Have partners discuss their reasoning and then share with the whole group.
Discuss the true/false questions.

Notes:

Decimal Multiplication & Division
Participant Assignments

1. **Read Chapter 1.**
   Are you a "Kim" or "Dana"? Describe your experience learning to compute. What parts of numeracy on p. 3 played a role in your experience? How do you think with numbers now? How do you do 7.02 − 0.97?

2. **Read Chapter 8 p. 105-106.**
   What are friendly numbers for decimals? How do these relate to money? What does it mean that, "students soon learn that they can use their whole number strategies with decimals, using place-value understanding to adjust the place value as necessary"? (p. 106)

3. **Read Chapter 10, p. 145-156.**
   Ask several people, including colleagues and students, "What is 16 · 0.26" Describe their responses, especially note if they use halves, quarters, or percents.

4. **Deliver the Power of a Tenth strings, p. 146.**

5. **Deliver the Multiplication Chunking strings, p. 147.**

6. **Deliver the Multiplication Over and Under strings, p. 148.**

7. **Deliver the Doubling/Halving string, p. 149.**

8. **Deliver the Division Chunking strings, p. 150.**

9. **Deliver the Division Over and Under strings, p. 151.**

10. **Deliver the Constant Ratio strings, p. 153.**

11. **Intersperse the strings with As Close As It Gets and Relational Thinking problems.**

12. **Look for opportunities to use the constant ratio strategy while doing the math at hand.**
    Force yourself to slow down and think about the numbers. Invite students to share moments of clarity when they apply numeracy and/or reasoning instead of rote memorization.

13. **Meet or beat the algorithm**
    Do you think you could always meet or beat the algorithm? If yes, invent multiplication and division problems for which you think you would meet the algorithm. If not, invent problems for which you think the algorithm is the most efficient strategy. What kinds of decimal problems do you think we could agree should be done with technology?

CHAPTER 9 nine 9

Percents

Percents

At a Glance

Materials

Blank paper, several sheets per participant

Large paper

Chart markers

Document camera

Projector

Big Ideas

Percents are ratios
Interpretations of rational numbers:
   Part-whole comparison, measurement, operator, quotient, ratio

Models

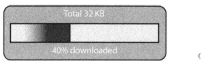

Strategies

The Golden Rule of Percent Bars (what you do to the number, you must do to the percent, and visa versa)

Preparation

- Read Chapter 1.
- Read Chapter 8, p. 115-120.
- Practice sketching models for each of the strings.
- Ask several people how they would find 70% off the price of $42, and note their responses.
- Ask several people how they figure a tip at a restaurant, and note their responses.
- Look in your textbook for typical percentage problems. Solve them using these strategies.
- Look for real opportunities in your life to find percentages using transparent strategies. Be prepared to share your experiences.
- Work the Comparing Strategies problems on percent bars and in ratio tables on your own.

Percents

At a Glance

Start Unknown

___ is 100 % of 40

___ is 200% of 40

___ is 50% of 40

___ is 25% of 40

___ is 10% of 40

___ is 5% of 40

___ is 1% of 40

___ is 6% of 40

___ is 0.5% of 40

___ is 13.5% of 40

___ is 24% of 40

___ is 85% of 40

p. 116

Percent Unknown

10 is what % of 20?

5 is what % of 20?

15 is what % of 20?

2 is what % of 20?

3 is what % of 20?

5 is what % of 50?

15 is what % of 50?

2 is what % of 50?

17 is what % of 50?

39 is what % of 40?

p. 116

Result Unknown

3 is 100% of ___

3 is 50% of ___

3 is 25% of ___

3 is 10% of ___

3 is 1% of ___

3 is 12% of ___

6 is 50% of ___

12 is 50% of ___

3 is 50% of ___

6 is 25% of ___

p. 116

The Commutative Property

35% of 20 is ___

20% of 35 is ___

60% of 15 is ___

15% of 60 is ___

22% of 100 is ___

100% of 22 is ___

44% of 25 is ___

25% of 44 is ___

36% of 75 is ___

21% of 33⅓ is ___

80% of 87.5 is ___

p. 134

Comparing Strategies

65% of ___ is 58.5

27 is 45% of ___

45 is ___% of 60

39% of 40 is ___

28 is 80% of ___

36 is ___% of 120

14.2 is 23.7% of ___

New

As Close As It Gets

8% of 12.5

a) 0.5   b) 0.75

c) 1.5   d) 2

24 is ___% of 32

a) 55   b) 66

c) 77   d) 88

New

Relational Thinking

Fill in the Blank:

31% of 50 = _% of 31

75% of __ = 24% of 75

True or False:

43% of 89 = 89% of _

3 is 12% of __ = 3% of 12

New

Using Ratio Tables

Workouts

Percents

Detailed Plan

Start Unknown

- **Deliver the extended ___ is 100 % of 40 string, p. 116**
- **Discuss Percent Bar Models**

FACILITATION TIP

Draw a large percent bar when you begin. Draw a long percent bar in order to represent the small relationships later in the string. Strive to make it as proportional as possible.

1. **Deliver the extended ___ is 100 % of 40 string, p. 116**
   Start with a giant empty percent bar.
   Write the problem to the left of the giant empty percent bar.
   For each problem, do the following:
   - State the problem.
   - Ask participants to label what is known.
   - Ask participants to answer the question.
   - Label the answer.
   - Discuss participants' reasoning.

   How did you find 5% of 40? How do you reason about it?

If a participants says this:	Model and restate:
I used 10%, which is 4. Since 5% is half of 10%, then 5% of 40 is 2.	 *Since you knew 10%, you could cut it in half to find 5%. Since you cut the percent in half, you cut its corresponding number, 4, in half to get 2.*

If a participants says this:	Model and restate:
I used the 50%, which is 20. Since 5% is ¹⁄₁₀ of 50%, then 5% of 40 is 2.
You already knew 50%, and you knew the relationship between 50% and 5%. So you found ¹⁄₁₀ of 50% by dividing by 10. Since you divided 50% by 10, you divided its corresponding number, 20, by 10 to get 2.
You could also use the 25%. Divide 25% by 5 to get 5%. Then divide 10 by 5 to get 2.
You know that 25% divided by 5 is 5% so you divided the corresponding 10 by 5 and also got 2. |

2. **Discuss Percent Bar Models**

    The models we choose are important. The percent bar works well because it begs for action. Once the given information is labeled on the percent bar, the student is looking at relationships. The task becomes finding other relationships that lead to finding the unknown.

Notes:

Percent Unknown

- Deliver the 10 is what % of 20 string, p. 116

1. **Deliver the 10 is what % of 20 string, p. 116**
   Deliver the string similarly to the start unknown string.

   How did you find 3 is what percent of 20? How do you reason about it?

If a participants says:	Model and restate:
I knew I could get from 20 to 1 by dividing by 20. So I also divided the 100% by 20 to get 5%. Then, I multiplied the 1 by 3 to get 3. So I multiplied the 5% with 3 to get 15%.	*You knew you could get to 1 from the total of 20 by dividing by 20. Then you only had to multiply by 3.*
I used the 15 that we already found as 75%. To get from 15 to 3, you divide by 5. So I divided 75% by 5 to get 15%.	*You already had 15 at 75%. To get to 3 from 15, you just divided by 5.*

Result Unknown

- Deliver the 3 is 100% of ___ string, 116
- Discuss proportional reasoning
- Name the strategy, and post it
- Discuss other percent solution methods

1. **Deliver the 3 is 100% of ___ string, 116**
   Deliver the string similarly to the start unknown string.

   How did you find 3 is 12% of what number? How do you reason about it?

If a participants says:	Model and restate:
First, I put everything down. Then I wondered how I could get from 12% to 100%. I knew I could divide 12% by 3 to get 4%. Then I could multiply the 4% by 25. So I did the same things to the numbers: divided 3 by 3 to get 1, and then multiplied by 25 to get 25. So 3 is 12% of 25.	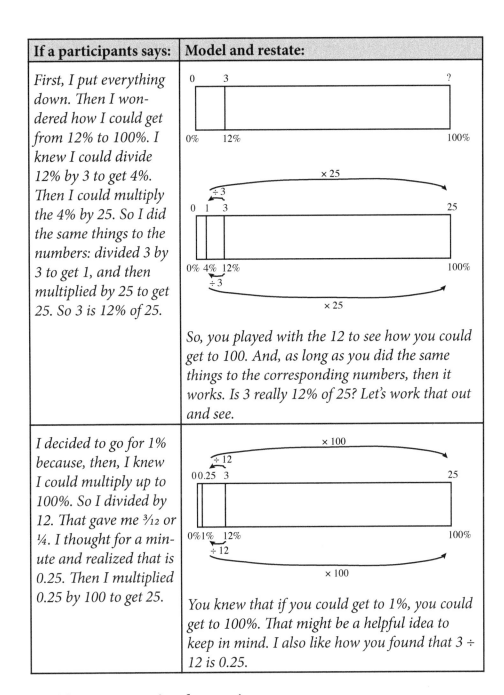 So, you played with the 12 to see how you could get to 100. And, as long as you did the same things to the corresponding numbers, then it works. Is 3 really 12% of 25? Let's work that out and see.
I decided to go for 1% because, then, I knew I could multiply up to 100%. So I divided by 12. That gave me ³/₁₂ or ¼. I thought for a minute and realized that is 0.25. Then I multiplied 0.25 by 100 to get 25.	*You knew that if you could get to 1%, you could get to 100%. That might be a helpful idea to keep in mind. I also like how you found that 3 ÷ 12 is 0.25.*

2. **Discuss proportional reasoning**

    Ask participants to turn to a partner and talk about the proportional reasoning that they used to solve these problems. Discuss the following as a whole group.

    How did you use proportional reasoning to solve these problems?
    How did you use the percent bar?
    What do you think about the idea that many of the problems have more than 1 way to solve them?

What do you think of using strings like these to deepen your students' intuitive feel for percent problems? ... and for their proportional reasoning?

3. **Name the strategy, and post it.**
   Ask participants to describe the strategy that most of them were using by the end of the string.

   Turn to your partner, and describe what you were doing every time.
   Try to generalize the kinds of things you were doing.
   Now, share your generalization with the group.
   What can we call this strategy to refer to this way of manipulating the numbers?

   Post the name and an example problem on large chart paper.

   Which problem in this string would you choose to represent what you are doing on the percent bar?

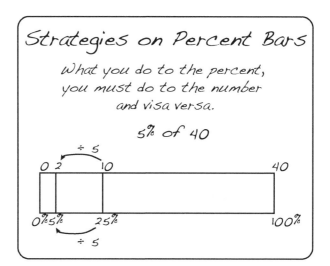

4. **Discuss other percent solution methods**
   Ask participants to turn to their partners and talk about how this compares to other percent solution methods:
   • setting up proportions, cross multiplying, and dividing
   • setting up equations and solving
   Bring the whole group together, and discuss.

   How does this percent bar proportional reasoning method compare with the solving proportions and cross multiply method?

   How does this percent bar proportional reasoning method compare with setting up equations and solving to find the answers to percent problems?

The Commutative Property

- **Deliver the 35% of 20 is ___ string in this guide**
- **Discuss the commutative property**
- **Name the strategy, and post it**

1. **Deliver the 35% of 20 is ___ string in this guide**
   The first problems in the string are paired problems whose answers are the same. In the first two sets of paired problems, neither problem is particularly easier than the other. Since the answers are the same, participants will begin to wonder why and if it happens all of the time.

   As participants solve each problem, ask for a couple of strategies to quickly share. Do not talk about the equal answers until you get to the third set, where the numbers are so easy that everyone will notice the pattern.

   > *Many of you are suggesting that 35% of 20 is equivalent to 20% of 35. Will this pattern continue?*

   When you ask, "44% of 25 is what?" some participants may immediately use the commutative property and find 25% of 44. If no one does, ask the next question, "25% of 44 is what?" and then discuss which of the two is easier to solve.

   > *Since we conjecture that we can use the commutative property to solve these percent problems, which would you rather solve? 44% of 25 or 25% of 44?*

   Finish the string with the last few problems. Have fun with last problem of finding 80% of 87.5 by finding ⅞ of 80.

2. **Discuss the commutative property**
   Have participants generalize what is happening.

   > *I see that many of you are convinced that n% of m = m% of n. Why do you think this is true? Convince me.*

   After discussing the generalization, ask participants to find their own clever problems for which using the commutative property turns a difficult problem into a easy one.
   Have each table contribute 2 problems to a group list posted at the front of the class. Have participants choose the 1 or 2 problems they think are the most clever.

3. **Name the strategy, and post it.**

Ask participants to describe the strategy that most of them were using by the end of the string.

> *Turn to your partner, and describe what you were doing every time.*
> *Try to generalize the kinds of things you were doing.*
> *Now, share your generalization with the group.*
> *What can we call this strategy to refer to this way of manipulating the numbers?*

Post the name and an example problem on large chart paper.

> *Which problem in this string would you choose to represent this percent swapping strategy?*

Percent Swapping Strategy

40% of $100 = 40$
100% of $40 = 40$
$n\%$ of $m = m\%$ of n
$(0.0n) * m = (0.0m) * n$
$(0.01)nm = (0.01)nm$

Using Ratio Tables

- **What about ugly problems?**
- **Try these**

1. **What about ugly problems?**

All of the problems in the strings have relatively nice answers. The answers are not all whole numbers, but all of the answers can be found using the numeric relationships and some clever proportional reasoning. What do we do about the honest ugly problems that we happen upon then? The point here is that, once students have constructed the relationships involved in percent problems, they will seek for clever ways to find the answers, and, even when they don't find one, they will know that they are trying to find a nice missing factor. They also will know that they are trying to find a nice way to multiply. When this happens, and no nice number is readily apparent, then participants can see what they need to do and will use ratio tables to get approximate answers to whatever level of precision they want.

2. **Try these**
   Ask participants to consider these problems:
   • What is 7% of 1.93?

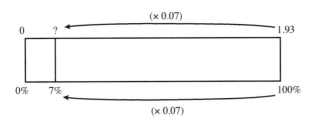

To solve, find 1.93×0.07.

   • 1.93 is what percent of 7?

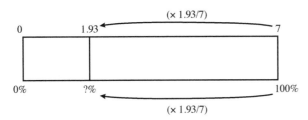

To solve, find $100 \times 1.93 \div 7$.

   • 1.93 is 7% of what number?

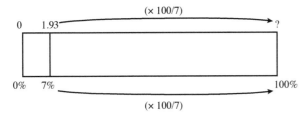

To solve, find $1.93 \times 100 \div 7$.

To do each of these calculations, use either a ratio table (see the section on ratio table multiplication and division), or use a calculator.

Comparing Strategies

Give participants the Comparing Strategies question in this guide. Circulate, and observe.

Ask a couple of participants to display their strategy for each problem. Discuss. Focus the discussion on what it is about the numbers that influences their strategy choice.

As Close As It Gets

Display the questions in this guide one at a time.

Ask participants to think quietly about the answer choice that is as close as they can get to the correct answer.

If time permits, ask partners to discuss their reasoning.

Ask a couple of participants to share their reasoning with the group. Remember:

- Show each problem one at a time.
- Discuss each before moving to the next problem.
- Don't just round. That answer may not be the closest.

Relational Thinking

Display the questions in this guide one at a time.

Ask participants to think quietly about the number that goes in the blank without computing. Suggest that they use relational thinking instead.

> Can you use relational thinking about how the numbers are related with that equal sign to fill in the blanks? Don't compute. Don't solve the equation; use the relationships to find the missing number.

Have partners discuss their reasoning and then share with the whole group.

Discuss the true/false questions.

Notes:

Percent Participant Assignments

1. **Read Chapter 1.**
   Are you a "Kim" or "Dana"? Describe your experience learning to compute. What parts of numeracy on p. 3 play a role in your experience? How do you think with numbers now? How do you find 55% of 22?

2. **Read Chapter 8 p. 115-120.**
   Ask several people, including colleagues and students, "How do you figure a fair tip?" Describe their responses.

3. **Display a typical download bar and discuss.**
   Ask your students where they see real percent bars. Ask students to present pictures of mp3 players, laptops, telephones, TVs, etc. where the picture shows a downloading bar. Discuss perceptions of percents in relation to what the bars indicate.

4. **Deliver the Start Unknown string on p. 116.**

5. **Deliver Percent Unknown string, p. 116.**

6. **Deliver Result Unknown string, p. 116.**

7. **Deliver The Commutative Property string in this guide.**

8. **Intersperse the strings with As Close As It Gets and Relational Thinking problems.**

9. **Look for opportunities to use each of the percent strategies while doing the math at hand.**
   Force yourself to slow down and think about the numbers. Invite students to share moments of clarity when they apply numeracy or reasoning instead of rote memorization.

10. **Find percent problems in your textbook or high stakes test**
    Try textbook or high stakes test percent problems using percent bars or ratio tables. Can you find problems for which neither percent bars nor ratio tables work? What is it about the numbers that make percent bars particularly nice? What is it about the numbers that make ratio tables a better model?

The Landscape of Learning

I draw largely on the work of Cathy Fosnot, Maarten Dolk, the Mathematics in the City group, and their combined work with Dutch researchers at the Freudenthal Institute, as published in the series Young Mathematicians at Work and Contexts for Learning Mathematics. These works build a framework for the teaching and learning of mathematics called the landscape of learning. What is the landscape of learning and how does it support our work with numeracy?

To understand the landscape of learning, let's first look briefly at what it is not. Most of us are taught in textbooks and by teachers a skill-based approach to math. This is a sort of linear trajectory: learn a skill, and then you are ready for the next skill. Each skill is necessary to learn the next, and you must follow this line of learning to keep moving toward higher math. Textbooks were written for classes where all students are ready for the same skill at the same level. But, now, we realize that all classes are multi-level with students all over the place. Stronger students become bored, and weaker students miss the mark because they can't even enter or access the problems.

In contrast, the landscape of learning is a developmental framework: less linear and more web-like and inter-connected. It is characterized by landmark mathematical ideas, strategies, and models. It depicts a learner's journey that is less prescribed and less focused on one and only one skill.

Consider driving down the road. You see landmarks all around you, in front of you, and on the horizon. Landmarks are also behind you. These are the big ideas, strategies, and models that you have already constructed; they are like tools in your tool box: your repertoire of things you can use to solve problems. The landmarks next to you close by are those that you are grappling with right now. The landmarks in front of you are outside of your primary focus, but you can see them in the distance. You are aware of them, and they might influence your work, but you are dealing with other landmarks directly. If you look way out in the distance, you can barely make out the landmarks on the horizon – these are the big ideas, models, and strategies that you can just glimpse and just begin to tinker with. As you grapple with the landmarks close to you, they are your focus. You might remember concentrating on one big idea yesterday, but it is now in your periphery and might get a little blurry.

Teachers often wonder why students seem to grasp a topic the day it is taught and then completely forget it soon after, but, to the student, those landmarks are still close by and still something to grapple with. The nearby landmarks shift in and out of focus. The more experience a student has with those big ideas, strategies, and models, the more the landmarks solidify and congeal. As this happens, the student moves along the landscape adding tools to the toolbox, and leaving those landmarks behind. The landmarks that were farther away are now coming into view. Now the student really starts to work with and to grapple with them. Also, those landmarks that were once way off on the horizon are now closer. New landmarks are beginning to appear on the horizon.

Algorithms

"Borrowing, carrying, and long division are algorithms that we learned to get answers to arithmetic problems. What is an algorithm? An algorithm is "a structured series of procedures that can be used across problems, regardless of the numbers." (Fosnot & Dolk, Constructing Multiplication and Division, 102).

"The algorithms ... that we teach in most schools today were invented by the great Arab mathematician, Muhammad ibn Musa al-Khwarizmi in the early part of the ninth century as an efficient computation strategy to replace the abacus. (In Latin his name was Algorismus – hence the term algorithm.) During this time, calculations using large numbers were needed both in the marketplace and for merchants' accounting purposes. Because calculations on the abacus were actions, there was no written record of the arithmetic, only the answer. And only the intelligentsia, practiced in the art of the abacus, could calculate. ... With the invention of the algorithms, and the dissemination of multiplication tables to use while performing them, even the most complex computations were possible, and written records of the calculations could be kept." (Fostnot & Dolk, Constructing Multiplication and Division, 97)

Algorithms are an important part of our history. They allow the common person to compute and to keep records. But, when faced with an arithmetic problem today, is it the right idea to perform a set of memorized steps, regardless of the numbers? When should we reach for a calculator? When should we use the relationships among the numbers in the problem to solve it in an efficient or perhaps even elegant way? What does it mean to have the number sense to find a good estimate or to evaluate the reasonableness of an answer?

Consider this problem: 1000 – 997. One can dutifully solve this problem using some 10+ steps by borrowing (regrouping) successively.

But, by allowing students to solve problems like these in their own way and then modeling, comparing, and discussing different strategies with the rest of the class, it honors the student's thinking and nudges the students toward more-efficient and sophisticated thinking. This is a different process that takes a student from where he/she is and provides experiences to nudge them toward more-efficient and sophisticated thinking while avoiding the mistake of superimposing an artificial construct that fails to connect to the student's level of thinking.

Here is a real-life problem that I (Pam) face once a month:

$$
\begin{array}{r}
1956.3 \\
98.97 \\
44.00 \\
+\ 89.99 \\
\end{array}
$$

Is this a realistic problem? It is actually 4 bills that I pay: credit card, mobile phone, gas, and cable. I have to make sure before I pay them, that I have enough money in the bank to cover the charges. How do I make sure? Do I line them up and start adding on the right? Do I pull out my cell phone calculator? Do I estimate? or use an exact amount?

Many adults and most children prefer to start with the largest amounts in a problem, until they have been taught the algorithm. Research shows that kids prefer to work big to small and left to right. Consider that, when you start with the largest number first, you already have a decent estimate.

Having a decent estimate means that a student is at least PDC (pretty darn close) because, if the student makes a mistake, the mistake is usually in the smaller numbers, and that translates to a smaller mistake. What about when kids use the formal algorithm? Where do they usually make their mistakes? In the ones? The tens? Students usually get the first few steps right, then they make mistakes in the hundreds and thousands: exactly the opposite of where you want the mistake.

This is true especially if it involves your bank account. How far off is the answer if you do what comes naturally and think big to small and make the error with the small numbers? Would you rather be off by a couple of dollars or by a couple of hundred dollars?

The standard addition algorithm is a fine thing for its original purpose: to add many multi-digit numbers accurately. The standard algorithm is not such a great tool to teach place value, number sense, and numerical fluency. The algorithm is one of the strategies a teacher should teach and that students should learn, but it should not be the first and certainly not the only strategy to use.

References

Fosnot, Catherine Twomey, and Maaren Dolk, 2001. *Young Mathematicians at Work: Constructing Multiplication and Division*. Portsmouth, NH: Heinemann.

Harris, Pamela Weber. 2011. *Building Powerful Numeracy for Middle and High School Students*. Portsmouth, NH: Heinemann.

Close to 100

Randomly choose 6 digits. Use 4 of them to form 2 two-digit numbers whose sum is as close to 100 as possible. Your score is the difference between the sum and 100.

			Sum	Score
1. _____	+ _____	=	_____	_____
2. _____	+ _____	=	_____	_____
3. _____	+ _____	=	_____	_____
4. _____	+ _____	=	_____	_____
5. _____	+ _____	=	_____	_____

Final Score _____

			Sum	Score
1. _____	+ _____	=	_____	_____
2. _____	+ _____	=	_____	_____
3. _____	+ _____	=	_____	_____
4. _____	+ _____	=	_____	_____
5. _____	+ _____	=	_____	_____

Final Score _____

Adapted from Grade 3 *Investigations in Number, Data, & Space*, Pearson

CPSIA information can be obtained
at www.ICGtesting.com
Printed in the USA
BVHW012017170519
548590BV00002B/31/P